G000164460

CHIANG MAI
& NORTHERN THAILAND

SUZANNE NAM

Contents

CHIANG MAI &
NORTHERN THAILAND

CHIANG MAI AND NORTHERN THAILAND

Distant mists, bird songs, and a distinct chill greet most mornings in the mountains and valleys of northern Thailand. Among the region's soaring peaks, lush jungles, and fertile plains you will find a patchwork of lifestyles still largely steeped in tradition. Agriculture, and more recently tourism, is the bread and butter here, and with everyone eventually congregating in the region's string of provincial towns there is a rich palette of culture, history, and adventure to experience. While modern first-class amenities can usually be found, the pace is relatively slow and the atmosphere relaxed, with the Thai word *sabai* (happy) often heard upon the lips of the local people and visitors.

With the exception of Chiang Mai itself, even the largest towns in northern Thailand are comparatively peaceful places, with smaller crowds and less traffic than other parts of the country. You will find a colorful array of mom-and-pop establishments, ranging from little bars and restaurants to boutique hotels and art shops, dotting the streets and keeping close company with produce markets, traditional medicine shops, and the hawker stands of the hill tribe people who come to sell their art, often dressed in their vibrant and elaborate ancestral costumes. Elegant spas, isolated resorts, sparkling waterfalls, and Buddhist temples spanning seven centuries add to the verdant tranquility on offer. Though you will find the various pit stops in this region woven together with a common thread of lifestyle, cuisine, and history, each locale has managed to retain its own unique character.

© SUZANNE NAM

HIGHLIGHTS

◖ Wat Chiang Man: Chiang Mai's oldest *wat* is also one of the best examples of Lanna-style architecture in the city (page 14).

◖ The Saturday Market: Excellent handmade goods, street snacks, and a relaxed vibe make for a perfect weekend afternoon in Chiang Mai (page 26).

◖ The Mae Sa Loop: Starting just outside of the city of Chiang Mai, this loop drive takes you to enchanted botanical gardens, small handicraft villages, and elephant camps, all set amidst rolling mountain scenery (page 49).

◖ Doi Mae Salong: Settled by fleeing Chinese soldiers, this town is a bit of China in Chiang Rai Province, with tea shops and Chinese temples (page 64).

◖ Mae Hong Son: This small border town, surrounded by mountains and jungle, offers plenty of opportunities to trek and explore without the crowds you'll find in Chiang Mai (page 67).

LOOK FOR ◖ TO FIND RECOMMENDED SIGHTS, ACTIVITIES, DINING, AND LODGING.

For travelers on a budget, the region can be a refreshing change from Bangkok and the islands, where the hordes of tourists seem to drive prices for accommodations, food, and transport higher and higher every year. Though northern Thailand is extremely popular with both international visitors and Thais on vacation, it remains an exceptional value destination.

PLANNING YOUR TIME

It's possible to experience Chiang Mai in just a few days, and if you don't mind limiting what you take in you could distill all of northern Thailand into a week. Of course you could also spend a month relaxing, trying your hand at any number of exotic and quirky activities, getting back to nature in steamy green jungles,

luxuriating at gorgeously appointed spas, taking in the rich mix of culture both in the villages and up on the mountains with the hill tribes—the list is almost endless, and in fact some people never go home! In other words, it's up to you. If you only have a few days you can easily fly into the town of your choice (for most people this is Chiang Mai), sign up for a quick jungle trek, visit the hill tribes, the zoo, a museum, and a few other key sights, and fly back out having sampled the best of the north and enjoyed a few exciting dining experiences to boot. It's also entirely reasonable to simply come out to enjoy the fresh mountain air and relative peace and quiet, doing nothing other than indulging in the good life at great prices.

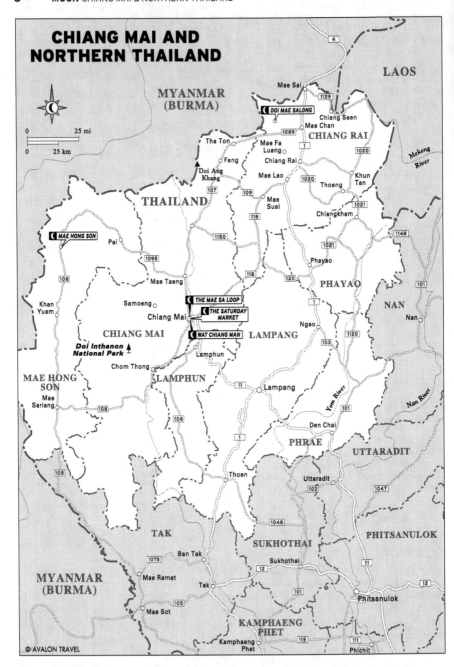

If you are ambitious and on a tight time budget, Chiang Mai makes a good base to sample the best the north has to offer. You can combine getting back to nature in the mountain jungles with visiting one of the most important temples in the region, Wat Doi Suthep, which is best seen at sunrise or sunset. Many who have gone before you would argue that if you skip the local elephant camps you've made a big mistake, so along with Doi Suthep head out to Mae Sa or one of the other camps in the area and see an eye-opening elephant show or even take a short swaying elephant ride through the forest.

The hill tribes, particularly the Long Neck Karen or Padaung, are not to be missed— their future is uncertain and you might not get another chance, so plan for a half day with them. This could be combined with a quick visit to some of the shopping areas located outside of town with their unique handicrafts and some of the best prices for souvenirs and local art in the country. Add to that a day starting with an early-morning foray to the Chiang Mai Zoo, a leisurely lunch, a quick trip to the National Museum, and an evening stroll to take in a few of the city's most lively and absorbing streets, ending with a cruise through the spirited Night Bazaar and a well-earned Thai beer of your choice. Of course, since the region is famous for elephants, you should probably order the Chang.

For those who become restless with too much relaxation, northern Thailand offers many exhilarating adventures set in the surrounding jungle; somewhere among the bungee jumping, trekking, mountain biking, elephant rides, and even light plane rentals, you are sure to find something to get your adrenaline up. Of course if that's not your scene, there is also plenty to keep history hunters, culture bugs, and shopping aficionados wide eyed and open mouthed for days on end.

Mercifully falling somewhere between a rural backwater and a world-class tourist zone, northern Thailand has all of the transportation benefits of a well-traveled resort area, with none of the big-city urban sprawl and traffic congestion. Networks of bus routes spider out from Chiang Mai to almost every northern town; many locales have airports and flights are short and generally inexpensive; dozens of organized tours cover the full gamut of local destinations, and reasonably well-maintained and intuitive road systems combine with cheap car rentals to make the north about as accessible as one could hope for. Most towns in the region are so small that walking to your destination is frequently a viable option, and when it's not taxis, *tuk tuks*, and *song thaew* (สองแถว) can usually be found nearby.

If you are seeking a more in-depth experience and have the time, consider enrolling in one of the surprising assortment of courses designed to provide you with a uniquely Thai experience and a one-of-a-kind souvenir: a new skill. Courses on offer last from a single day up to a week or more, and cover such exotic subjects as *muay Thai* boxing, Thai cookery, traditional dance, meditation, massage, traditional arts, and even opportunities to become a "certified" elephant mahout. Prices are generally very reasonable by Western standards and some include room and board.

HISTORY

To visit northern Thailand is to step into the ancient kingdom of Lannathai, whose name means The Land of a Million Rice Fields. For centuries the Lanna Kingdom was the northern counterpart to the Siamese Kingdom of Sukhothai to the south. While a cultural and territorial tug-of-war between Siam and Burma held the kingdom in its cross-hairs for centuries, Lannathai eventually became the loyal and integrated part of modern Thailand that you'll see today. However, the northern Thais still see themselves as distinctly different from their southern compatriots and indeed have a history and ancestry all their own.

While there is evidence that the mountains and valleys of northern Thailand have been inhabited for at least 2,000 years, the cultural roots of the current residents began in the 6th century when the Mon people made their way through the forests from what is now Myanmar (formerly called Burma). Drawn

brick *chedi* in Chiang Mai's old city

by trade to the fertile valleys and rivers, they created their capital at Haripunchai, the city now known as Lamphun. Spreading insatiably across Thailand, Laos, and into Cambodia over the following 400 years, they brought cultural and artistic influences that are still in evidence today. Most importantly, it is believed that they introduced Buddhism to the region, a thread that is deeply entwined with the daily lives of residents even now, 1,500 years later.

The Lanna Kingdom was the creation of the young King Mengrai, 13th-century ruler of the people living in what is now the southern Chinese province of Yunnan and the northern sections of Myanmar, Laos, and Thailand. Born in Chiang Saen, he set about to unify the people scattered throughout the region under his banner and in 1262 founded Chiang Rai, the capital of his new kingdom, which he named after himself. Ambitious and charismatic, he did not stop there. Pushing south he expanded his territory through conquest and persuasion all the way through the intervening Mon settlements to the borders of the

Sukhothai Kingdom of southern Thailand. After annexing Haripunchai, King Mengrai felt that his kingdom needed a strong city in its new territories. After inviting his friends the kings of the Sukhothai and Payao Kingdoms to inspect a verdant plain near the Ping River and to help him build a city there, in 1296 Nopburi Sri Nakorn Ping Chiang Mai was founded. Each of the three kings made a small cut in his wrist and spilled blood into a silver chalice; each then drank from the cup and vowed everlasting support to one another. Whether the consumption of blood played a role or not, there were no wars between the three kingdoms during the reigns of these men. A statue was erected for the three kings and can still be found in the city (on Intawarorot Rd., at the corner of Phra Pinklao Rd.), whose name was later shortened to Chiang Mai, which means simply "New City." Near the three kings statue in the center of the old city there is a shrine to King Mengrai. According to legend it stands in the spot where he was struck by lightning and killed in his 80th year, concluding his life with a ferocity that seemed to match the passion with which he had lived it.

Strategically positioned on the trade route between the Yunnan Province and the ports of Burma, the Lanna Kingdom flourished and experienced a golden age of prosperity through the 15th century, expanding its territory to include most of northern Thailand, large tracts of Myanmar and Laos, and a small part of southern China. Chiang Mai became the capital in 1345 and in 1477 was the site of the Seventh World Buddhist Conference. Unfortunately, finding itself surrounded by hostile neighbors in Burma, Laos, and the Ayutthaya Kingdom that had replaced the Sukhothai Kingdom to the south, the Lanna Kingdom was weakened by conflict in the 16th century and swayed between independent control and foreign occupation. In 1558 Chiang Mai fell to Burmese forces and for the following two centuries was exploited as a key military base in their campaign against Ayutthaya. Finally the Lanna people allied themselves with the Siamese forces and drove out the Burmese, but the city was left in such a state of devastation that it was completely abandoned in 1776 for 15 years with the capital shifting back to Lamphun, the original Mon center.

It was King Rama I of the current Chakri Dynasty who resurrected Chiang Mai; he reestablished leadership for the region in the form of a princehood awarded to a former military leader. The new prince then went on to encourage repopulation by the peoples who had become spread out and disorganized during the conflict years. This firmly established the northern provinces as the loyal part of Siam that they are today. Finally, the addition of the railway built in 1921 opened up the north to the rest of the country, providing access both to natural resources such as teak and farmland, and to the villages for migration and tourism. The last 20 years have seen enormous growth in these mountain towns, whose relative isolation was so complete until so recently that the imprint of isolation continues to be felt, for now at least.

Chiang Mai เชียงใหม่

Despite its status as one of the country's largest cities and its population of 1.5 million people, Chiang Mai has managed to hang onto its small-town feel even as it developed into a modern center. Even though it boasts the biggest hotels, flashiest night spots, and the bulk of tourist services in northern Thailand, as you cruise the city's ancient streets and wander through its wealth of temples you may find yourself wondering where these 1.5 million people are. In fact the population is spread out around the city's periphery, but after spending a few days in the area you might think the right answer is at the markets. Shopping draws Thais and tourists alike to Chiang Mai, and its markets are the heart of local activity. This of course means more foreigners and slightly higher prices than you'll find elsewhere in the north, but even at these elevated levels both remain very reasonable. Seven hundred years of history has left a perceptible footprint here that can be felt in the *wats,* religious icons, antiques shops, and ancient structures, such as the remains of the old city walls that still serve, along with the original moat, as the border of the town's heart.

SIGHTS

Chiang Mai, the regional urban center and the largest city in the north, abounds with international flavor, modern conveniences, respectable infrastructure, and well-developed tourist attractions. While these are certainly a comfort to travelers, what makes the city so special is the subtlety with which these have been blended with the rich cultural history, natural beauty, and agrarian way of life that preceded them by so many centuries. Here you can visit mysterious ancient temples, trek through mountainous rain forests, hunt among antiques and a wealth of local products for that perfect memento, indulge in world-class pampering in one of the lavish spas, and then settle in for a sumptuous dinner and fancy cocktails with live music by the river, all in the space of one day. Of course no one will blame you for setting a more relaxed pace if you prefer!

Wats

Even the most modest of after-lunch strolls about the streets of Chiang Mai is bound to find you skirting past monks and shielding your eyes as the sun glints off mirrored tiles adorning one of the incredible 300 *wats,* at least as many as sprawling Bangkok claims, that garnish every corner of this city. Cool green meditation gardens, shining pagodas, exotic statues, and Buddha images of every size and description await your exploration with a welcoming vibe unique to the houses of Buddhism. Although you are clearly spoiled for choice, don't assume that sheer volume means these temples are more or less clones of one another.

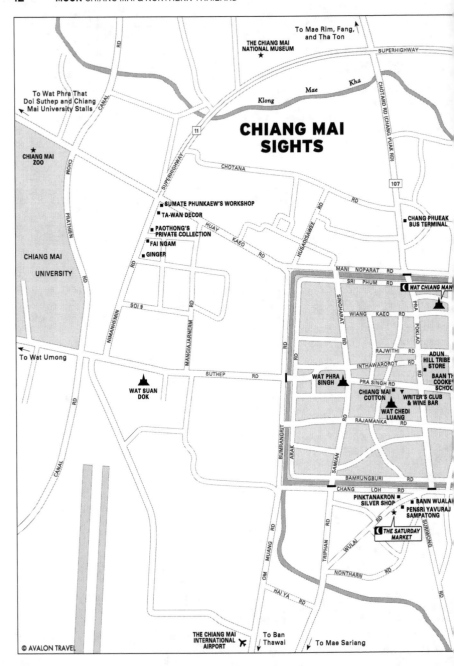

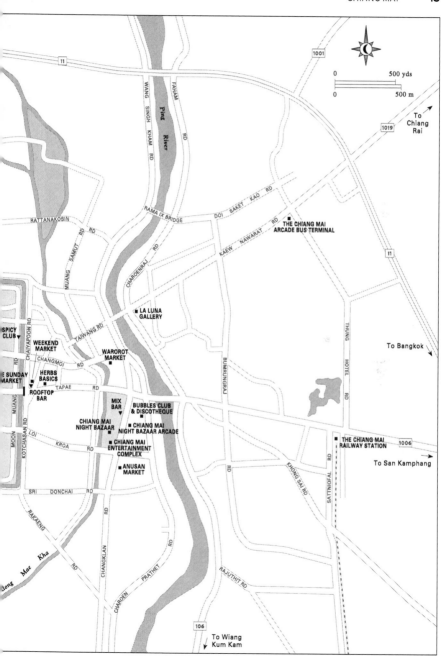

© SUZANNE NAM

Detailed reliefs adorn many of Chiang Mai's temples.

There is a surprising variety on offer with some featuring vivid murals, others mysterious relics, and a few even have small museums of Chiang Mai history. Far from being shrouded with indecipherable *darmas* (rules of Buddhism) guarded by stern, tight-lipped priests, these gleaming compounds often employ displays that seem almost designed to speak to those with no knowledge of the teachings or of the language that they are written in. There are a few that are particularly notable, but wandering into any one that you come across might reveal an arcane tidbit or rewarding cultural experience and leave you feeling just a little bit more enlightened.

If you want to spend a bit of time checking out the temples, you can cover a few of the best by following a simple route starting at Chiang Mai's oldest temple, **Wat Chiang Man** in the northeast section of the old city, then heading south to **Wat Chedi Luang,** and after that striking out east to hit **Wat Phra Singh, Wat Suan Dok,** and finally **Wat Umong.** While you won't really be able to claim that you've seen all there is to see in Chiang Mai templery, you will

get a nice overview touching on a few things that are really unique and important, and have a pleasant half-day excursion in the process.

◖ WAT CHIANG MAN
วัดเชียงมัน

Wat Chiang Man (171 Ratchaphakhinai Rd. near Chang Phueak Gate, Si Phum subdistrict, tel. 05/337-5386) was built in 1292 and is Chiang Mai's first and oldest temple; it is believed that King Mengrai lived here while he was planning and building the city. In fact a stone tablet found at this site tells the story of the city's founding and was used by historians to place the date of the city's construction. The tablet can still be seen on the outer wall of the ordination hall at the northeast corner of the compound. Chiang Man is an excellent example of a *wat* decorated in the Lanna style, as seen in its red roofs, abundance of red lacquer, liberal use of gold leaf, and multicolored tiles of mirrored glass. One of the best-loved features of this temple is its unusual elephant pagoda, consisting of a bell-shaped *chedi* drenched in

© SUZANNE NAM

A novice monk cleans the steps at one of Chiang Mai's golden *chedis*.

gold leaf and supported on a base of plaster elephants facing outward on all sides, which is the oldest structure in the compound. Even more venerable, however, is the *wiharn* at the north end of the compound, easily recognized by the particularly beautiful *nagas* (mythical snakes) adorning the stairs and roof and sparkling in mirrored finery. This building houses two very ancient and sacred Buddha images; one is the marble Buddha bas-relief that it's believed was created in Sri Lanka about 2,000 years ago. It has a reputation as having the power to bring rain, and so is paraded around the city during Songkran to protect against drought. The other is the 1,800-year-old crystal Buddha that was relocated from Lopburi and is believed to protect the city against disaster.

WAT CHEDI LUANG
วัดเจดียหลวง

South on Phra Pinklao Road (also called Phra Pokklao Rd.) at the intersection with Ratchamanka Road is the 600-year-old Wat

Chedi Luang (tel. 05/327-8595), or The Royal Pagoda, as well as a more modern temple in front of it. The ancient *chedi*, with its surrounding elephant statues and *nagas*, looks very old and mysterious, due in part to the fact that it is only partially restored. It was probably the tallest and most impressive of the city's *wats* at one time; no one is quite sure how it was destroyed. Some theories include earthquakes or cannon fire, but since there is no consensus on what it originally looked like, work on putting it back together has never been completed—which only adds to its charm. Chedi Luang is also famous for having once housed the Emerald Buddha that is now on the must-see list of attractions in Bangkok. A jade Buddha now sits in its place here.

WAT PHRA SINGH
วัดพระสิงห

On your short trip east to Wat Phra Singh (Singharat Rd. at Ratchadamnoen Rd., tel. 05/381-4164), you'll see many little cafés where you can get iced coffee and snacks or stop for a beer. Visiting the temples requires a fair amount of walking and it can be uncomfortably hot and sunny in some parts of the compounds, so if you need a pit stop this area is a good choice. Once you arrive at the *wat* it's a good idea to take your time, as Phra Singh is one of the more enjoyable temples to stroll around. In the entrance to the grounds there are people selling souvenirs, water, and snacks if you didn't have time to stop on the way over or just happen to want some ice cream.

What makes this one of the most important of Chiang Mai's 300 temples is the Phra Singh Buddha image for which the *wat* is named. It is located in the *wiharn* behind and to the left of the main temple building, although even without the relic this *wiharn* would be enough to put Phra Singh on the map. Its three-tiered roof is a wonderful example of Lanna architecture, and the beautifully detailed gold tracery and carvings found in its gables and veranda are worth closer inspection. When you head inside you will see the bronze cast **Phra Singh relic,** whose name means "Lion Buddha." This

murals at Wat Chedi Luang

image is the most sacred of all of Chiang Mai's Buddhas and is important because it combines elements from Indian religious art styles with the usual Sukhothai style common for this period, which is very rare. It's thought that Lanna artisans must have seen examples of the Indian style carried by travelers and set about incorporating it into their own works. Looking at the image you can see that the Buddha is a little plumper than most you'll see, and that he sports a lotus on the top of his head (meant to be a flame). There are only a handful of examples in this genre remaining and no one is sure which, if any of them, may be the original that inspired the brief Lion Buddha trend. Before you leave the *wiharn*, take a moment to enjoy the murals depicting scenes from the Lanna court as it was in the early 1800s when the paintings were done.

Although completely lacking any historical significance, one fun and quirky feature of Wat Phra Singh is its rather unique meditation garden, which commands a large section at the rear of the compound. Not only are the shade and an opportunity to sit and relax for a

moment a very welcoming prospect, but a stroll along its path yields the tranquil garden backdrop that you might expect, and a little something extra. As you move about you will notice that a variety of wise sayings have been posted on the trees, and they're even in English. You will find a few that may put a smile on your face, such as "There is no glory for a lazy person, no matter how good looking," and a few that might leave non-Buddhists a little puzzled, such as "The best revenge is to end revenge." Walking among the trees bearing lessons in this quiet natural setting creates a pleasant vibe that is not difficult to pick up on.

Wat Phra Singh is one of the Chiang Mai temples that supports Monk Chat, a free program designed to provide visitors a chance to better understand what goes on at the *wats*, while giving the monks an opportunity to practice their English. You can ask them any questions that you want, from what it's like to live in a monastery to what the meaning of life is, although they are still working on their English, so they might stumble a little with their answers. For an outsider it's a great

© SUZANNE NAM

monks at Wat Chedi Luang

way to see the human side of the saffron-robed monks that we unconsciously tend to give a wide berth; for the most part you will find them to be open and friendly, and by no means above occasionally dissolving into the giggles.

WAT SUAN DOK AND WAT UMONG
วัดสวนดอกและวัดอุโมงค์

If you haven't had your fill of temples by this point, you might want to hire a taxi to get to Wat Suan Dok and Wat Umong, which are both outside the old city walls. **Suan Dok** (tel. 05/327-8967) or Wat Buppha Ram (วัดบุปผาราม) is located on Suthep Road, west of Suan Dok Gate, and while it does have some interesting history, its claim to a much more eerie feature is what sets it apart. Before Wat Phra That Doi Suthep (described later in this chapter) was built, this temple was home to a very important Buddha relic and was the location of the apparent miracle that inspired the monarchy to build a special *wat* to honor and house the relic (Wat Doi Suthep). The "eerie" attraction here is the unusual aboveground cemetery that is home to the cremated remains of members of Chiang Mai's royal family, a feature found in very few locations throughout the country. Although this collection of white-washed monuments might strike you as something you'd expect to see in an old mausoleum back home, walking among them you see that the style is clearly Thai. The monuments are mostly miniature *chedi* of various sizes and descriptions and you will notice that people still actively come to the site to pay their respects by laying lotus flowers and other offerings at the markers.

Wat Umong (Soi Wat Umong, Tambon Suthep, tel. 05/327-3990), or "Wat Tunnel" in Thai, located near the base of Suthep Mountain, is a little off the well-beaten path and it can be a bit of an adventure to get to it, but its well-deserved reputation for being the most unusual temple in Chiang Mai makes up for it. To get there you need to follow Suthep Road west over the Chonlaprathan Canal and then pass through a rabbit warren of small roads that make up a small local community. There are signs, but unfortunately not always where you need them, although driving through this community with its tiny shops and houses is interesting in itself. Once you have arrived you might think that you are in the wrong place because the compound looks nothing like a typical *wat;* what you are looking for is the raised mound with a *chedi* on top, which you will find heading left from the parking area. Wat Umong is basically a man-made mound of dirt criss-crossed with a small network of tunnels. Legend suggests that the *wat* was built to accommodate a monk that was so in touch with the Buddha that he was a bit out of touch with the world around him. The mad monk was highly revered but had an unfortunate tendency to wander off, so they built the tunnels to make it difficult for him to find his way out, though no one today knows how well it worked.

Wat Umong was abandoned for many years and only came back into use in the 1940s; as a result much of the sprawling grounds are overgrown and well forested, which adds a lot of charm to the site. Simply walking along the tranquil paths and down to its lake while gazing at the flowers and butterflies is quite a treat. People come here to meditate in peace and quiet and you will probably see the odd acolyte in yoga gear sitting under a tree. After you have explored the tunnels and climbed to the top of the mound to visit the *chedi* and take a few photos, walk around the base of the mound and investigate the outbuildings. As you go you will see the broken Buddha repository where people leave their old and broken icons and offerings to honor them; the rows of damaged statues creates quite an effect. Among the modern buildings next to the mound is a spiritual theater of paintings where local artists have decorated every available surface with murals depicting their contemporary take on Buddhism. Most of these murals are as different as night and day from the usual temple art, and you will see interestingly rendered scenes attempting to portray everything from the peace of meditation to philosophies on race relations in a variety of styles.

temple detailing on a *wat* in Chiang Mai

OTHER *WATS*

If you have time to take in a few additional *wats* while in Chiang Mai, you're in luck— there are hundreds of them to choose from. Though they may not be as historically or architecturally relevant as those listed above, if you are in the area they are worth at least a few minutes of your time.

Wat Jed Yot (วัดเจ็ดยอด, Chiang Mai–Lamphun Rd. at the intersection of Huay Kaew Rd. betw. Rtes. 1004 and 107, tel. 05/321-9483), a few kilometers northwest of the city, is one of the oldest and most historically significant *wats* in Chiang Mai. Built in the 15th century for the World Buddhist Council, the *wat* is loosely based on the Mahabodhi Temple in India, where the Buddha embraced the "middle way," the heart of Buddhist philosophy. The temple is named for its seven peaks, but unfortunately these spires and the rest of the stone structures have not been restored and remain in a state of disrepair. Despite their age and condition, there are still some beautiful

sculpted human figures on the buildings worth close inspection.

Just off of Tha Phae Road between the moat and the river, at the end of a narrow alley, is one of the city's loveliest unsung *wats*, **Wat Saen Fang** (Tha Phae Rd. just before Chang Moi Tat Mai Rd., no phone). The Burmese-style *wat* is worth a visit for its elaborately decorated *chedi*, a multileveled white stepped *chedi* leading up to a golden spire. The center of the *chedi* is covered in multicolored tiling and the three-tiered effect of the combination of white stone, colored tiles, and gold is unique in Chiang Mai. The *wiharn* and *ubosot* are both red wooden structures with elaborate painted gold panels.

On the east bank of the Ping River is **Wat Ket Garam** (betw. Charoen Rat Rd. and Na Wat Ket Rd., no phone, museum 9 A.M.–5 P.M. daily, donation appreciated), a fascinating *wat* with some interesting features. The most striking, and rarest, is the five-gabled *wiharn*. The five stepped roofs give the illusion that there are five prayer halls in succession instead of just one; this is not something you'll see in any other *wat* in the city or perhaps even in the country. The white *chedi* itself is not particularly interesting, but there the small museum in the *wat* complex is worth visiting. Though there is some Buddhist paraphernalia, the collection of old photos of Chiang Mai (with subjects both secular and sectarian) spanning more than a century is a real find.

One of the quirkiest *wats* in Chiang Mai is **Wat Wela Wanaram** (corner of Chotana Rd. and Ku Tao Rd., tel. 05/321-1842). Most of the buildings that make up this 17th century complex are not extraordinary, but the *chedi* is a series of five balls that diminish in size as the *chedi* climbs to the sky. The *wat* is also known as Wat Ku Tao, which means watermelon *wat*, although many visitors find it looks more like a series of gourds or balls than watermelons. Historians are not sure who built Wat Wela Wanaram or why the *chedi* looks the way it does, as there are no others like it in the country. Some speculate that it was built by Yunnan Chinese, others by Burmese.

The Chiang Mai National Museum
พิพิธภัณฑสถานแหงชาติเชียงใหม่

The Chiang Mai National Museum (Chiang Mai–Lamphun Rd., tel. 05/322-1308, www.thailandmuseum.com/thaimuseum_eng/chiangmai/main.htm, 9 A.M.–4 P.M. Wed.–Sun., 30B) is your best bet for getting a little bit of background to put your visit to northern Thailand in context. Home to a wonderful collection of ancient jewelry, 14th-century kilns, ancient art and Buddha images, and traditional weaponry, this stylish and well-organized attraction will lead you through the basics of Lanna culture and allow you to see past the modernized towns into the long history of development in the region. On a hot or rainy afternoon in particular the museum provides a few very comfortable hours of sightseeing and education. It's not advisable to walk along the superhighway, so get a taxi or *tuk tuk* from the center of town; there should also be a few waiting nearby once you are ready to return.

The museum's facilities were renovated and upgraded for the city's heptacentennial in 1996 and you can see this reflected in the well-designed exhibits and displays. As you approach, take a moment to appreciate the architecture of the main building, which is a grandiose reproduction of a traditional Lanna-style house, including a very elaborate example of the classic roof. There are six themes or topics meant to be followed in chronological order, and navigating the museum is made very easy by the visitor-friendly signs and English-language information plaques associated with the displays. Each topic is well organized into its own wing of the building and as you set out you will pass through the area dedicated to the region's natural and cultural background and earliest history. After that continue to the period from Chiang Mai's establishment to its capture by the Burmese; and then to the period where Lanna became a part of Siam.

The 2nd floor deals with art and modernization and offers an interesting assortment of ancient farming equipment along with an excellent collection of photographs. Your first exhibit is in the north wing and focuses on a brief history of the Lanna Kingdom's trade and economy from the late 1700s to the early 1900s, which marked the beginning of the end for many traditional systems. You will then pass through the section dedicated to the modern way of life along with information on contemporary social, agricultural, and economic management. The final exhibit is one of the best and covers the development of the Lanna art style and the history of art in Thailand. The collection boasts some very ancient and beautiful pieces such as 14th-century San Kamphaeng ceramics, and 15th-century Lanna Buddha images that have made their way here from religious sites and private treasure vaults throughout the region.

ENTERTAINMENT AND EVENTS
Bars

A very popular nightspot among locals and visitors is the atmospheric **Riverside Bar and Restaurant** (9–11 Charoenrat Rd., tel.

05/324-6323, www.theriversidechiangmai.com, 6 P.M.–1 A.M.). Scoring big points for ambience, this three-level open-air establishment is all teakwood and lanterns with live music and fairy-tale views overlooking the river and the old city on the other side. On the main level the band, the bar, and the majority of the crowd sets the stage, but you can choose the lower level right next to the river, or the upper level with the best view for a quieter, more intimate setting. The transition from restaurant to bar begins when candlelight and soft instrumental gives way to up-tempo acoustic and eventually live Western rock and pop all the way until closing time at 1 A.M., with the generally large and welcoming crowd laughing and singing along right until the end. You can order the usual beer and highballs, but a nice selection of wine and cocktails are also available at reasonable prices, and can be ordered in small, medium, and large carafes that are perfect for sharing.

Just a short way up the same street is **The Brasserie** (37 Charoenrat Rd., tel. 05/324-1665, 6 P.M.–1 A.M.), which distinguishes itself with live jazz and unique decor. Less crowded and a bit quieter than the Riverside Bar and Restaurant, The Brasserie is also located on the river and has a look all its own. Gauzy lanterns, lush greenery, and rugged woodwork give this place a funky tropical feel, keeping things fun without sacrificing sophistication. Drinks are a little more expensive here than at the Riverside, but getting to drink them in the soft light cast from paper lanterns shaped like giant mushrooms has a transporting effect that offsets the slight price difference.

For a break from exploring the streets at the night market, the **Chiang Mai Night Bazaar Arcade** (just off of Chang Khlan Rd. north of Loi Khro Rd., 6 P.M.–1 A.M.) is a good bet for a relaxed drink. It's a small section in the heart of the night market where you can choose from a number of little bars that spill out onto the sidewalks and run together creating a big open area that hums with activity for your casual drink under the stars. There are quite a number of these little places standing side by side on the arcade and they usually draw a lot of people without being crowded. There isn't a whole lot of variation between them, so just pick the one that seems to have the best crowd and that is playing music you like. If you feel like a little free entertainment, position yourself where you can get a good view of "The Wall," the massive climbing facade that looms up as you approach the arcade. You can watch the youthful bravado of the local daredevils as they compete for vertical mastery with no safety equipment of any kind. For a small fee you are welcome to give it a try for yourself. Its location among these little bars makes for a frightening combination of alcohol and daredevilry. There are also a number of bars in behind The Wall if you don't see anything you like out front. The places in this area are open until 1 A.M. and are great for inexpensive drinks and interesting people-watching.

Another similar venue, although perhaps a bit darker and stranger, is the **Chiang Mai Entertainment Complex** (east of the Night Bazaar off Loi Khro Rd., no phone). You'll find about 25 bars around the edges of the large complex with open fronts and indoor/outdoor seating and the same variety of cheap drinks. In the center is a *muay Thai* boxing ring where star pupils from the CEC Thai Kickboxing School and Gym display their skills in staged fights. Though it's not the real thing, they're still pretty convincing and you get to see some of the moves used in real fights. Occasionally other forms of entertainment show up in the complex, including cock fights. As with the kickboxing, it's less vicious than the real thing, and it's interesting to see how they care for the birds and prepare them for the fight. Afterward people will come around for optional donations in support of whomever put on the show you just watched. Most of the places in the Chiang Mai Entertainment Complex are open until midnight but hours seem to be a little faster and looser here.

While it probably won't be most people's favorite scene for an evening drink, you can have a completely bizarre experience at the **TCH Rooftop Bar** (19/4-5 Kotchasarn Rd., tel. 05/320-6886). Even though it's a reggae bar, "TCH" in this case doesn't stand for the active component in marijuana, but rather "Tribal Heritage Conservation." You will find a hemp shop on the main level as you go in; after that you start up a steep, narrow staircase on your way to the rooftop bar. About halfway you have to take off your shoes; take care not to toss them into what becomes a giant pile of footwear as the night heats up—place them somewhere you can find them, and be careful not to drink so much that finding them and making your way down these slightly scary stairs will be a problem. When you make it to the top you will find yourself in a rooftop Rasta den packed with character, though perhaps not really Thai character. Looking around you'll see mellow multicolored lanterns and fairy lights, street art done in glo paint sprawling over the walls, and not a chair in sight. Instead pockets of low tables and reclining cushions pepper the hardwood floor. This bar is partially uncovered, and you have the opportunity to lounge under the stars or gaze out at Suthep Mountain, with Wat Doi Suthep shining over the city during the day, and the golden electric glow of Tha Phae Gate in the evening. Attracting a large young bohemian crowd from all over the world, there is a very friendly atmosphere here and it's a good place to meet people. There is no cover charge and drinks are fairly inexpensive; you can order cocktails by the bucket if you're up to it. While this place looks for all the world like the sort of spot that will be treated to a police raid at any moment, everything appears to be on the up and up—there is no visible drug use here. You can also sample vegetarian snacks, or take a vegetarian cooking class, as you might expect in a place like this; handmade tattoos are also available.

More refined cocktail and wine bars can be found at some of the upscale hotels, such as the generally subdued and inexpensive **Writer's Club & Wine Bar** (141/3 Ratchadamnoen Rd., tel. 05/381-4187, noon–midnight Sun.–Fri.), where you can order basic cocktails, exotic import beers, and carafes of wine with your cheap but tasty plate of Thai traditional snacks. The name sounds a bit pretentious, but in reality the mood is friendly and the venue quieter and more civilized than most places in its price range, although the decor is fairly plain except for the small outdoor seating area.

The Dusit D2, a very plush hotel under the Dusit Hotels and Resorts umbrella, boasts one of Chiang Mai's trendiest nightspots. The **Mix Bar** (D2 Hotel, 100 Chan Klan Rd., tel. 05/399-9999, 6 P.M.–1 A.M. daily) located in its lobby mixes cocktails and some very creative martinis, which are served alongside light snacks. Billing itself as "defying all style genres," the mood is sort of ultra-mod lounge-y with an open floor plan, soft imaginative lighting, and an eclectic mix of furniture. It's the place to sip a lemongrass-and-ginger martini while breaking in any chic new fashion pieces that you've picked up in the city's high-end boutiques.

Nightclubs

This is one area where there is sadly very little to choose from in Chiang Mai. If you feel like dressing up and going dancing, or if you just want a fancy drink and some incredibly entertaining people-watching, **Bubbles Club & Discotheque** (Pornping Tower Hotel, 46–48 Charoen Rd., tel. 05/327-0099, 7 P.M.–late, 100B cover includes one drink) is your best choice. With its hip modern interior, huge drink menu, and DJs spinning some very respectable contemporary dance tunes, it's a wonder this place isn't dangerously crowded. Though it does pick up momentum as the night whirls on, you'll never find yourself lacking enough room to break out your favorite dance moves. The bar only takes coupons, so purchase them at the window next to the bar and then exchange them for the drink of your choice from the impeccably dressed bartenders. Anyone should feel accepted here among the delightfully eclectic crowd—from Chiang Mai's hippest young locals, to elderly package tourists and ultra-cool same-sex couples, it would be difficult to feel shy among this group. Even if you just sit back and enjoy the show you can bet on a fun night out.

If it's after 1 A.M. and you're just not ready to

stumble back to your hotel, you can head over to **Spicy Club** (82 Chaiyaphun Rd., alongside the Moat, opposite Somport Market, tel. 05/323-4860, 7 p.m.–1 a.m. daily, no cover). Somewhere between a bar and a nightclub, it does have a bit of dancing and not a whole lot else to recommend it. It is however where everybody in Chiang Mai goes for a late-night, or early-morning, drink and is the only place that is open after 1 a.m. It's dark and usually crowded; most people arrive here already intoxicated and young locals dominate the scene. Drinks are cheap and the music runs a fairly broad spectrum, so if you feel like the night is still young and everything seems to be closed, do what everyone else does and head to Spicy.

Festivals and Events

Chiang Mai is home to a handful of fun and festive events throughout the year, the most popular being the celebration of the national New Year holiday, Songkran. Timing for all of these events varies from year to year; make sure to check with the Tourism Authority of Thailand (105/1 Chiang Mai-Lamphun Rd., tel. 05/324-8604, 8:30 a.m.–4:30 p.m. daily) for specific dates.

Coinciding with the tourist high season, in late December and early January the city hosts a **Cool Season Fair** in the area surrounding the Tha Phae Gate. The year-round market atmosphere becomes even more intense, and the number of food and handicraft vendors grows exponentially during this time.

The **Flower Festival,** held in February, is a three-day event with a flower show and a parade where you'll see elaborately and colorfully decorated floats making their way through the city. In addition to the flowers, there are live-music performances, dance performances, and plenty of eating and shopping.

Songkran, the celebration of Thai New Year in mid-April, gets particularly intense in Chiang Mai. Here instead of the normal three days, the city has stretched it out to five days of water-soaked celebrations.

Loi Krathong, celebrated in late October or early November, is perhaps the country's most beautiful holiday, made even more visually stunning in Chiang Mai. On Loi Krathong, everyone buys or makes a *krathong*—a small float covered with flowers and candles—and launches it out onto the river in the evening, resulting in thousands of lighted floats on the water. In Chiang Mai, they also launch large translucent paper hot-air balloons that light up the skies. The festival, with roots in Hinduism and Buddhism, has taken on additional meaning in modern times. The release of the *krathong* symbolizes the letting go of anger, grudges, and bad luck and the atmosphere during this holiday is particularly cheerful and friendly.

SHOPPING

It has been said that visitors to Thailand should wait until they get to Chiang Mai to do their shopping, and with good reason. Considered one of the major traditional art centers of Asia and well known for its enticing bargains, Chiang Mai is a favorite shopping destination for Thais, tourists, and even international dealers. From street stalls to upscale art and antique dealers, you'll find silks, silver, ceramics, lacquerware, clothing, interior decor, art, rattan, and of course all of those little souvenir knickknacks for the people back home. Many high-quality items are available, but cheaply made goods and fakes are also easy to find, so examine the products carefully. Shoppers looking just to take home some handcrafted housewares and accessories are really in luck here, as prices for these items are generally very reasonable and the quality high. If you've bought too much, don't worry. You'll also have no trouble finding extra suitcases and even shipping services to help you get that four-foot wooden elephant carving home.

Clothing and Fabrics

For stunning silk and cotton togs, don't miss world-class designer Sumate Phunkaew's workshop **Classic Model** (95/2 Nimmanhemin Rd., tel. 05/321-6810, www.cm-fashion.com). Though his fashions are displayed in Bangkok, Chiang Mai is his home and Sumate's work

© SUZANNE NAM

Chiang Mai abounds with handmade goods.

is avant-garde, imaginative, and quite Thai in flavor, allowing you to find something that's both chic and totally unavailable back home.

For trendy, eye-catching designs in clothing and jewelry, visit **Ginger** (6/21 Nimmanhemin Rd., tel. 05/321-5635), where you will find cuts and colors waiting to jazz up your collection. Featuring off-beat stylish pieces, this shop specializes in well-designed tunics and funky accessories.

A wonderful collection in an exciting array of fabrics can be found at Ajarn Paothong's breathtaking shop named, quite simply, **Paothong's Private Collection** (4 Nimmanhaemin Soi 1, tel. 05/321-7715). As well as showcasing Paothong's exceptional designs, this three-story Chinese-style house also displays a variety of interesting artifacts and pieces from his collection of vintage fabrics, all of which inspire his work.

A first-rate designer of men's fashions is found at **Fai Ngam** (Apt. E, Nimmanhemin Soi 1, tel. 05/322-1130) where Khun Noi's extraordinary hand-stitched work can be bought off the rack or commissioned for custom pieces.

He specializes in cotton pieces; the magic is in the cut and in the details of his creations.

In the same building as Ginger, **Living Space** (276–278 Tha Phae Rd., tel. 05/387-4299) has got possibly the best collection of lacquerware in Chiang Mai, made special by its array of unexpected colors in pieces gathered from Thailand and Vietnam. Far from being limited to the traditional dark tones, there is a rainbow of vibrant hues ready-made to fit into any decorating scheme.

Chuck your way through mountains of hill-tribe fabrics at **Adun Hill Tribe Store** (210/1 Phra Pokklao Rd., tel. 08/943-4141, www.adunhilltribe.com). The store sells clothing and accessories (shoulder-slung bags, embroidered belts, even thong sandals) all made by hill tribes such as Hmong, Akha, Shan, Musser, Yao, and the long-necked Padaung. Nearly all of the fabric is hand woven or embroidered and much of it is vintage. Ask the owner, who was born in an Akha village and designs some himself, about the villages he procures the goods from.

For those who like cute boutiques,

SONGKRAN FESTIVAL IN CHIANG MAI

If you are lucky enough to be visiting Chiang Mai in mid-April, you will find yourself in the best location in Thailand to enjoy the raucous fun of the ancient festival Songkran. Originally the new year's celebration of the Tai people, Songkran is older than Thailand itself and is considered a time to honor your family, community, and religion, and to show respect for water, the most important element in the agricultural lifestyle of so many people of the region.

Despite such a noble pedigree, the festival is probably most famous for its reputation as a giant three-day nationwide water fight. Visitors can expect to find themselves right in the middle of three full days of ritual merrymaking and celebration. The spectacle of the people participating in the antiquated Songkran rituals is not to be missed, but do not get your hair done in the days leading up to the festival — simply leaving your hotel room guarantees that you are going to get very wet. The water fight is a sort of natural extension of the bathing ceremonies at the heart of the Songkran merit-making rituals, and you will see this theme on all three days of the festivities.

The first day, Maha Songkran, symbolizes the end of the old year and usually falls on April 13th; if you sleep late don't be alarmed by the crack of explosions beginning early in morning — it is simply the local people lighting firecrackers in an attempt to chase off the bad luck of the previous year. In Chiang Mai there is a procession of floats and Buddha images beginning at Nariwat Bridge and winding its way to Wat Phra Singh. People will usually also clean their homes, bathe, and wear new clothes on this day.

Wan Nao or Wan Da is Preparation Day, the second day of the festival. People will set to work preparing a variety of offerings to honor Lord Buddha. Head to the Ping River in the afternoon to see people gathering sand to be used in the building of sand stupas, which will be richly decorated with colorful flags and flowers and presented to Lord Buddha at the temples later that day.

Day three, Wan Phaya Wan or Wan Taleung Sok, is the actual first day of the new year. Go to the temples to see offerings of food and other gifts made to the monks, and the Tan Kan Kao, the honoring of elders and late ancestors with offerings of food and well wishes. This is followed by the unusual ritual of using sticks and branches to prop up Sri Maha Bhodi trees, made famous for their reputation as

---

Laddawan's (25/2 Ratwithi Rd., tel. 05/341-8999, laddahamric@yahoo.com) is full of fun clothes and accessories. They carry modern and ethnic goods as well as modern styles made from traditional textiles. They have a nice selection of jewelry too and everything is made in Thailand. If the shopping has exhausted you, go upstairs for an inexpensive massage.

Chiang Mai Cotton (141/6 Ratchadamnoen Rd., tel. 09/757-5659, www.chiangmaicotton.com) is a chic boutique selling all goods made from exquisite cotton in many styles of tops, pants, skirts, and dresses. They also carry accessories and jewelry. If you want to order large quantities wholesale, they are equipped to export and you can create your own styles. There are also locations at the Kalare Night Bazaar (Room D146) and the new Northern Village at the airport (Room 012A, 1st fl.).

Textile House (85 Kumpang Din Rd., tel. 05/320-6819) has a wide selection of gorgeous Thai and Lao silks and cottons. Their prices are excellent, and although the shop is small it has a funky, tribal atmosphere. They also have an ample number of ethnic textiles such as Hmong batik, and embroidery as well as other ethnic handicrafts. A great find of a store.

Arts and Handicrafts

If it's art you're looking for, **La Luna Gallery** (190 Charoenrat Rd., tel. 05/330-6678, www.lalunagallery.com) has two stories of Thai, Burmese, and Malaysian contemporary works available for purchase. Not limited to

being the tree that Buddha was sitting under at the moment he became enlightened. Weave your way through the crowds and simply take in the kaleidoscope of activity as people continue to make merit by setting captive birds and fish free, and by bathing Buddha images with sweetly scented water. The young will also bathe the hands of their elders and ask forgiveness for past misdeeds in the Rot Nam Dam Hua ritual. There will be a procession of traditional dancers in native costume and beautifully arranged flowers, in which water is poured on respected monks and high-ranking government officials. Unique to the northern provinces, the stupas containing the ashes of ancestors will also be bathed in order to pay respect and receive forgiveness.

The festival is set in April as a result of a meeting of the Tais' rich agricultural identity with the importance of rice sowing and harvesting cycles to their daily lives, and the strong astrological associations that Buddhism inherited from Brahman India. The Tais originally placed Songkran in late November, a time of harvest in southern China where they lived. As they migrated south into what is now Thailand, these cycles were adapted to the warmer, more tropical climate, although there are a handful of rural people who keep with tradition and still celebrate Songkran in November. As Buddhism captured the hearts of the Tai people, auspicious movements of the heavenly bodies that coincided with the April harvest were discovered, and also played a role in setting the date. In fact the term "Songkran" means "a move or change in the position of the sun from Aries to Taurus." Even today the position of the sun and the phase of the moon still give the last word on what exact date Songkran falls; it may occur anywhere between April 10th and 18th, although the buzz of excitement precedes the event for days.

If you're in Chiang Mai, or any part of Thailand, during this period, stores and shops will be closed, and at the height of the festival it may appear that order has completely broken down. The streets will be teeming with people of all ages, toting high-pressure water guns and buckets of water. You'll even see kids piled into pickup trucks cum mobile watering units complete with 10-gallon drums of sometimes icy water. And no one will shy away from dousing you just because you are a tourist. Locals take precautions such as stashing their mobile phones in plastic baggies, and you probably should too.

---

paintings, they also sell an abundance of furniture and ceramics in a wide range of styles and prices. With the size of this collection, it's handy that their website includes a comprehensive catalog of what's available for those can't afford to spend hours wandering around the large gallery.

Ta-Wan Decor (1 Nimmanhemin Rd., tel. 05/389-4941) features an interesting assortment of unique home-design items made from mango wood that is smoked and then dyed; pieces are accented with threads of native fibers in stylish designs. This one-of-a-kind technique won't be found in the markets or in any of your favorite shops back home.

Loi Khro Road, which leads up to the night market, has a string of woodcarving, sculpture, "antiques," and textile shops. Many do wholesale as well. Alongside them are streetside massage parlors if you want to take a break, and a couple of shops worth noting. **Kukuwan Gallery** (37 Loi Khro Rd., tel. 05/320-6747) has a wonderful collection of silk and cotton goods. Everything is handmade and colored with natural dyes, and almost all come from villages in Chiang Mai Province. The quality is superior and the pieces are beautiful. Make sure to look at the ceramics as well.

Beauty Products

Herbs Basics (172 Klang Wiang Intersection, tel. 05/323-4585 and 172 Papok Klao Rd., tel. 05/341-8289, www.herbbasicsproduct .com, 9 A.M.–8 P.M. Mon.–Sat., 1–8 P.M. Sun.)

offers high-end chic toiletries and spa/beauty products at surprisingly reasonable prices. The number of scents is practically endless and you can cut your own soap bar for 0.50B/gram. They also sell things in multiple sizes, which is great for traveling; many products are priced at 50B or 100B. Don't miss their peppermint herbal body scrub, and for those with sensitive skin, their glycerin soap (the vanilla is a particularly nice one). They have many accessories as well, and will make up a gift package for you—wrapping is free.

Markets

Market shopping in Chiang Mai is like no other part of the country. If you decide to hit all the markets in the area, you'll need at least a few solid days to see everything on offer.

CHIANG MAI NIGHT BAZAAR
เชียงใหม่ไนท์บาซาร์

The best known of Chiang Mai's markets, the Night Bazaar is a kaleidoscope of color, activity, and bargains. Located right in the heart of the city on Chang Khlan Rd., hemmed in by Chiang Mai Road to the north and Loi Khro Road on the south, the market begins to stir in the early evening and hums until midnight. You can go into the actual three-story Night Bazaar building, or simply prowl the little shops that pour out all over the road. A must-see for most visitors, shoppers will delight in the sheer number of heavily laden street stalls displaying all kinds of woodcrafts, paintings, textiles, jewelry, clothing, ceramics, and much, much more. Even the non-shoppers will enjoy the amazing congregation of people from all over Thailand and the rest of the world, not to mention the many little spots to stop for a snack or a beer, perfect for watching the commotion in relative comfort. If you're a discerning shopper you may find lots of cheap crafts and knock-offs. Better to continue onto the pleasant and spacious **Anusan Market,** or the pavilion housing **Kalare Bazaarr/Food and Shopping Center** in the center of the bazaar, where you can find higher-quality goods, or do as the trendy visiting Thais do and schedule your visit around the weekend markets.

THE SUNDAY MARKET
ถนนคนเดิน

The Sunday Market (Ratchadamnoen Rd., 2–10 P.M. Sun.) is one of the bazaars that has made Chiang Mai famous among travelers, and this is definitely a gaze-and-saunter experience. The market spans many streets and many come here from around the region to sell their goods, which include everything from cute silk-screened T-shirts to hand-woven baskets. You will also see shops around town with stands, and there is original artwork as well. It's a great place for small gifts, although it can be difficult to make decisions, as there is so much around! It is also popular with travelers from within the country and there is often some sort of performance or other spectacle going on to further add to the eye-candy quotient. Bring your wallet as well as your appetite—there is enticing street food all around.

◖ THE SATURDAY MARKET
ถนนคนเดิน

More relaxed and less "business-like" than the Sunday market is the Saturday Market (Wualai Rd., 5:30–10:30 P.M. or later Sat.). It has many small producers selling their wares, from sandals made from local plants to silk scarves and wood carvings. Although there's plenty of inexpensive stuff to lug back home, some of the pieces are definitely higher quality. Bargaining is expected, but the prices are already very reasonable because of the competition. This market is often the favorite of the repeat visitors to Chiang Mai, and locals will typically recommend it as the best of its kind in the city. A couple of shops to check out include **Pensri Yavuraj Sampatong** (tel. 08/1681-0687); look for her on your left as you walk down from the old city; her woodcarvings are hand-done and very detailed. **Pinktanakron Silver Shop** (4–8 Wualai Rd., tel. 05/327-1768) is on your right just at the start of the road. Their jewelry is what really catches your eye, but they also have housewares: bowls, platters, and even purely silver handbags. The ornamentation is superb and everything is quality silver. They also have some antiques and do wholesaling and goods made to order. **Bann Wualai** (118–120 Wualai Rd., tel. 05/320-3055, www.bannwualai.net) is definitely worth a visit if you are in the area. Marketing itself as carrying "authentic hill-tribe, Thai, and Burmese crafts," it's much like an old basement, chock-full of old antiques and hill-tribes relics, old tools, and bamboo buffalo sacks. Make sure you look upwards—they have a host of things lining the ceiling. If you are interested in fabrics/textiles, make sure to ask for them—many are stored in the cabinets.

WEEKEND MARKET
ตลาดนัด

Selling similar goods, but a bit quieter and more relaxed, is the Weekend Market running on Sunday just outside the Tha Phae Gate. Prices here are sometimes even better than at the Night Bazaar, and although there is less to choose from, the market is a bit more open and less claustrophobic, sometimes spilling into nearby temple compounds. It's open after 3 P.M. until midnight; often vendors are easier to bargain with toward the end of the evening. And of course you will find local food, cafés, and places to refresh yourself with an icy beer should the shopping become too much for you.

WAROROT MARKET
ตลาดวโรรส

If you want to have a day out for your senses rather than for your pocketbook, consider spending some time in one of the more traditional markets. Warorot Market (7 A.M.–4 P.M. daily), between Chang Moi Tat Mai Road and the Ping River, offers a feast of brightly colored fabrics, flowers, fresh food, and traditional medicines; stroll among the vendors and simply take in the sounds, sights, and aromas of a traditional Thai market. Don't forget to keep an eye out for things you've never seen before, and for that perfect photograph.

Antiques

With 700 years of history and an entire kingdom gone to dust under its feet, it's no surprise that Chiang Mai is considered an antiquing hot spot. You can find everything from

ancient Buddha images and other religious relics to time-worn opium paraphernalia and antique jewelry laid out for you in high-class shops and portable street stalls. While it is possible to pick up something truly special for a song, you need a practiced eye to avoid the fakes and illegal items that are sometimes sold at the markets. Genuine pieces should come with a certificate from the National Fine Arts Department, but it's important to note that no sacred Buddha images (as opposed to reproductions), new or antique, can be legally removed from Thailand without obtaining permission. All images created for a specific religious purpose fall under this category, despite what dealers may tell you.

There are a handful of dealers along Tha Phae Road, and there are some reputable shops on the upper level of the Night Bazaar, but by far the best selection and best prices will be found at Ban Thawai. Even window shoppers will enjoy gazing at the broad selection of antique pieces and simply wondering at their past. There's furniture, farm tools, glass, stone and wood carvings, and statues of bronze, brass, copper, pewter, and porcelain—even if you are not a collector there is a good chance that you will find something to capture your imagination.

RECREATION
Thai Cooking Schools

The popularity of Thai culinary classes is well earned not only because they can be a lot of fun and are a great place to meet people, but because of the undeniable appeal of being able to go home and create savory mementos to remind you of your trip and wow your friends. Chiang Mai has an impressive concentration of cooking courses available both inside the city and in outlying areas, and although not all are created equal many of them are very well put together. The best classes offer not only cooking instruction but a trip to a local wet market to select ingredients. It's almost worth the tuition simply to go to market with a local person and have them finally explain some of that strange-looking Thai produce to you, as well as how to go about

khao soi, the region's signature dish

choosing the best specimens among them. Fees also generally include all the menu expenses, a lift to and from your hotel, a Thai cookbook that you can keep, and of course lunch—once you are finished stirring, chopping, and simmering you'll be able to sit down and judge your creations for yourself. Since many of the schools offer small classes, it's important to book your lesson at least a couple of days in advance.

With its handy location right in town near the Tha Phae Gate, **Baan Thai Cookery School** (11 Rachadamnern Soi 5, tel. 05/335-7339, www.cookinthai.com) runs classes each day of the week, keeping them to intimate groups of less than ten and setting a friendly and casual atmosphere. The classes each fill an entire day, and teach a variety of menus featuring classic Thai favorites. The classes include basics like making the different curry pastes and important Thai sauces, and a highly enlightening trip to the local market to pick up the ingredients for the day's cooking. And if you find yourself two months later stuck trying to remember the correct method for crushing coriander or braising bamboo shoots, you can take advantage of

their offer of free lifetime Thai cooking support by email; of course you'll need to give them a couple of days to get back to you, so make sure to contact them well before that fancy Thai dinner party if necessary.

Chiang Mai Thai Cookery School (47/2 Moon Muang Rd., tel. 05/320-6388, www.thai cookeryschool.com) is one of the most popular cooking schools in the region and offers one-to five-day group courses in traditional Thai cuisine, as well as individual training for more accomplished chefs. If you take the full week of classes, you'll learn everything from making your own curry paste to traditional fruit-carving techniques in addition to instruction on how to create Thai dishes such as pad thai and *tom yam kung.*

If you prefer organic ingredients, the **Thai Farm Cooking School** (2/2 Ratchadamnoen Rd. Soi 5, tel. 07/174-9285, www.thaifarmcook ing.net) offers lessons on their organic farm just outside the city. Though you'll select some of your ingredients from the local market, you'll also get to tour the farm and see how local vegetables and herbs are grown. The full-day course will have you preparing at least four dishes and all of the instruction is hands on.

Spas

Chiang Mai has scores of day spas and massage parlors if you're looking to relax sore muscles after some hiking or just indulge after some shopping. You'll find a good selection across price ranges, and except at the absolute top end, you'll find services in general to be less expensive than in Bangkok. If you're just looking for a basic massage at one of the many small massage parlors, expect to pay between 200 and 400B for an hour. If you want a real spa, a 60- or 90-minute massage will cost anywhere from 600B and up. Hours vary; call for an appointment at the following establishments:

Ban Sabai Spa (17/7 Charoen Prathet Rd., tel. 05/328-5204, www.ban-sabai.com) is conveniently located for those staying in the old city and has nicely furnished, comfortable treatment rooms. The spa is not over the top, but a pleasant, reasonably priced place offering typical services. This is a very popular spa with tourists.

Spa Mantra (30/11 Chareun Suk Rd., tel. 05/322-6655, www.spamantra-international.com) is another good mid-priced day spa. Treatments get creative and seem to often involve food products—there are yogurt, wine, coffee, sesame, and rice treatments, but if you're not up for a scrubbing or detox treatment, the basic massages are good too. The exterior of this spa is not particularly stunning but the treatment rooms themselves are nicely decorated.

Sinativa Spa Club (22/1 Nimanhemin Soi 9, tel. 05/321-7928, www.sinativaspaclub.com) is in a wooden house off of Nimmanhemin Road and offers plenty of typical spa treatments, including facials, scrubs, wraps, and of course massage. Although the spa is not amazingly fancy, the setting is relaxing and tranquil and the treatments are reasonably priced. They also offer pickup and drop-off from your hotel if it's too far to get to on foot.

For a slightly more medical approach, the **Rarinjinda Wellness Spa and Resort** (14 Charoen Rat Rd., tel. 05/324-7000) offers treatments in their modern spa/resort near the river. The focus here is on wellness, but if you just want a massage or scrub they will happily oblige.

Chur Medical Spa (102 Sirimangkalajarn Rd., tel. 05/323-3923) focuses even more heavily on wellness and "science" (though you may be skeptical after hearing their claims about their cellulite treatments) but doesn't completely forgo comfort and pampering. Some treatments are targeted towards slimming, firming, or holistic health but there are also regular massages available.

At the top end are the **Four Seasons Spa** (Mae Rim-Samoeng Kao Rd., tel. 05/329-8181, www.fourseasons.com) and the **Dheva Spa** (51/4 Chiang Mai-San Kamphaeng Rd., tel. 05/388-8888, www.mandarinoriental.com) at the Dhara Dhevi Mandarin Oriental. The Dheva is particularly striking—the spa grounds are on a re-created temple and all of the private treatment rooms are large and luxurious. Both have won international recognition for their services and decor and are priced accordingly.

If you'd like to learn massage instead of getting one, the **Thai Massage School of Chiang Mai** (203/6 Mae Jo Rd., Mu 6, T. Fa Ham, tel. 05/385-4330, www.tmcschool.com) and the **Thai Massage School** (238/8 Wualai Rd., tel. 05/320-1663, www.thaimassageschool.ac.th) offer one-week and longer courses. Though these are very well priced (less than 10,000B for a full two-week course), both are professionally run programs with classroom and hands-on components. They are designed for local and foreign massage therapists and those just interested in learning Thai massage techniques.

ACCOMMODATIONS

A hugely popular tourist town for both local and international visitors, Chiang Mai is full of places to sleep. Inexpensive guesthouses geared towards backpackers and large, sterile hotels once dominated the scene here, but increasingly there are excellent mid-range small hotels available for those who want to enjoy some of the charms of the city without having to rough it, as well as some amazing resorts just outside

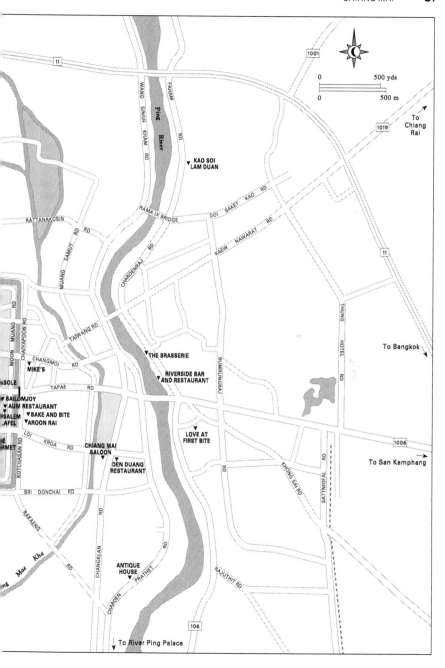

of the city. If you're picky about where you stay, and don't want to be bothered by touts or have to carry your bags around as you hunt for a place to stay, book ahead. Many of even the most inexpensive guesthouses have websites, making it simple to inquire about availability and make a reservation before you arrive. If you are coming during high season in December and January, or around the Songkran and Loi Krathong festivals, you must book ahead. If you are planning on doing any hiking or visiting the hill tribes, your hotel or guesthouse will be able to arrange the excursion for you; many even have tour agencies attached.

Under 1,500B

It's cheap, charming, and well located—no wonder the **Julie Guest House** (7/1 Phra Pokklao Soi 5, tel. 05/327-4355, www.julie guesthouse.com, 300B) is everyone's favorite budget accommodation in the city. Rooms are small but colorful and clean and there are hammocks and small corners of the common areas in which to lounge around and read a book or enjoy a cup of coffee. The guesthouse is just a few minutes' walk from the Tha Phae Gate, inside of the moated old city. The price quoted is for a double room with fan and a private bathroom with hot water. There are also dormitory beds available for 50B per night. There is an inexpensive massage parlor next door run by the same people, as well as a travel agency that can arrange hiking trips.

Another nice, inexpensive guesthouse inside the old city is **Bow Chiang Mai House** (15 Moon Muang Soi 9, tel. 05/321-1707, www.bowchiangmaihouse.com, 400B). The building is a little more modern than the typical wooden houses many cheaper accommodations in the city inhabit. Though not particularly stylish, the rooms are comfortable and clean, and the staff is friendly and helpful.

In a prime location, **Parasol Inn** (105/1 Phra Pokklao Rd., Klang Wiang Intersection, tel. 05/381-4011, www.parasolinn.com, 850B) is a modern hotel with breakfast included. Rooms are very well kept and have cable TV and fridges/minibars. This is a great inexpensive

option but note that only the top-floor rooms have windows.

West of the moat in the Nimmanhemin area is **Baan Say-La** (Nimmanhemin Rd. Soi 5, tel. 08/6911-1184, 900B), a small, stylish boutique guesthouse with well-furnished rooms in a white colonial-style wooden house. Though the decor is a blend of traditional colonial and Thai styles, the photography and modern art on the walls give the property a modern edge. There is a comfortable common sitting area and kitchen if you'd like to prepare your own meals.

Buri Gallery House (102 Ratchadamnoen Rd., tel. 05/341-6500–4, http://buri-gallery-house.th66.com, 1,000B) is a newer hotel in an amazing location—in the center of the old city. Housed in a beautifully made Thai-style wooden house made into a small modern hotel, some rooms are very small but the service is excellent. Breakfast is included and they have an outside seating area. There is a massage parlor right in the lobby and Internet is free if you need to check email.

Maa-T-Nee (74/4 Viengkeaw Rd., tel. 08/9757-1161 or 05/341-6243, 1,200B) is in the northwest corner of the moat. This modern guesthouse is bright and clean although basic. There is a café downstairs and the stone walls make a cool atmosphere. Wi-Fi is available.

The top-notch charming service and beautiful lobby send many visitors home happy after staying at ◖ **3 Sis Bed & Breakfast** (1 Phra Pokklao Soi 8, tel. 05/327-3243, www.3sisbedandbreakfast.com, 1,300B); it makes for a pleasant stay right in the old city and a block away from Wat Chedi Luang. A very chic café serving Thai and Western dishes (with ingredients from the father of the three sisters' organic farm) is downstairs. Rooms are very comfortable, the bathrooms particularly lavish for the price, and there's free Wi-Fi throughout the hotel. Although a newer place, it already has garnered passionate reviews and in 2008 they finished a new wing with 24 more upscale rooms. Considering that breakfast is included and the place is run very professionally, with completely modern amenities, the price is more than worth it.

1,500-3,000B

Just out of the center of town on the Ping River, the **River Ping Palace** (385/2 Charoen Prathet Rd., tel. 05/327-4932, http://river pingpalace.tripod.com, 1,500B) is a great little guesthouse for those looking for something a little quieter. The small complex of old wooden houses is decorated with antiques and the breezy dining area overlooking the river is a lovely place to enjoy a slow breakfast before heading out to see the sights. Rooms are comfortable but very basic, as are the bathrooms. You will feel like you're staying in an old house, for better or worse.

Just outside of the city on the east side of the Ping River, ◖ **Baan Orphin** (150 Charoen Rat Rd., tel. 05/324-3677, www.baanorphin.com, 1,900B) is a lovely little hotel with rooms and private bungalows, all done in teakwood with traditional Thai decorations throughout. The grounds are luxuriant and there's even a swimming pool, a rarity in this price range. Four-poster beds and airy verandas make Baan Orphin a great place for couples looking for a tranquil, romantic getaway, but the larger suites are good for small families too.

A must for the upscale bohemian traveler, **Villa Duang Champa** (82 Ratchadamnoen Rd., www.villaduangchampa.com, 2,200B) is a newer addition, right behind the Three Kings' Monument. In an exquisite top-notch refurbish of a breezy antique building, each room is unique and simply a pleasure to enter. Style is tasteful and plush yet simple. All rooms have flat-screen TVs and some have bathtubs. Original artwork is on display in the sun-filled interior where you take your breakfast, which is included. There's also Wi-Fi.

3,000-4,500B

All of the individually designed, comfortable rooms at **Tea Vana** (75 Chiang Mai–Lamphun Rd., tel. 05/330-2805, www.tea-vana.com, 3,200B) have a slightly Chinese feel to them, but the real theme here is tea. Each room is named after a tea; there are even tea-based treatments at the adjacent spa. This small, chic boutique hotel is located on the Ping River and there's also a swimming pool and a restaurant/café.

Tri Yaan Na Ros Colonial House (156 Wualai Rd., tel. 05/327-3174, www.triyaann aros.com, 3,500B) is a truly different kind of hotel, which takes great pride in its traditional blend of architecture that captures the "proud history of Chiang Mai." Tri Yaan Na Ros has a bit of a homey, bed-and-breakfast feel, as it is small but the rooms are still totally luxurious and the setting a blissfully secluded, quiet interior. Breakfast is included in the rate, and is best taken by the tranquil pool. Besides a small dining room they have an interesting gallery of many arts and antiques from northern Thailand and the region; ask to be shown. Service is impeccable. It was the 2004 winner of the Best Conserved Structure Award by the Lanna Architect Association.

Over 4,500B

◖ **Tamarind Village** (50/1 Ratchadamnoen Rd., tel. 05/341-8896, www.tamarindvillage .com, 6,000B) is an oasis in the middle of the old city, a boutique hotel set in a large walled-in green space that somehow manages to create an aura of true peace and quiet right in the middle of backpackers and *tuk tuks*. Rooms are rustic in that they have more classic than modern design elements, but they're also spacious, clean, and luxuriously appointed. Tamarind Village is often booked months in advance, especially around holidays.

If you are looking for absolute luxury, the **Four Seasons Chiang Mai** (Mae Rim-Samoeng Kao Rd., tel. 05/329-8181, www.fourseasons.com, US$400) has enormous stand-alone villas set on a green rice paddy. Although the property is outside of the city, there is a daily shuttle to the center and plenty of activities such as cooking classes and even a rice-harvesting class to keep you busy if you stay there.

The **Mandarin Oriental Dhara Dhevi** (51/4 Chiang Mai-San Kamphaeng Rd., tel. 05/388-8888, www.mandarinoriental.com, US$450) is a resort that's been designed to make you feel as though you've stepped back a few centuries into a Lanna Kingdom palace. The architecture of all of the structures interwoven among the property's rice paddies is northern Thai, Shan,

© SUZANNE NAM

typical outdoor market in Chiang Mai

or Burmese and the effect is stunning. This is the most beautiful resort in northern Thailand. Rooms and villas are very spacious and have individual outdoor lounge areas. There is also an expansive (and expensive) spa on the premises.

FOOD

Chiang Mai has scores of restaurants to choose from, and the variety of options available is second only to Bangkok. Here you'll find typical guesthouse fare, restaurants geared towards Western tourists, traditional Thai food, and a lot of vegetarian options. Because Chiang Mai is such a tourist town, it's hard to find places to eat that don't attract other visitors, so don't be dismayed if you're eating with travelers from around the world. It usually doesn't mean the food isn't authentic, but rather that it's good.

Markets and Food Stalls

At any of the shopping markets in the city there will also be plenty to eat, from mango sticky rice to fruit shakes to *khai nok kratha,* or fried quail eggs served in little banana-leaf baskets. Most of what you'll find is meant to be eaten on the go, to keep you energized while you shop, but there is also more substantial fare available. The **Chiang Mai Night Bazaar** has food stalls interwoven with the crafts and trinkets, including lots of *satay* and even *khao mok gai,* chicken and yellow rice. **Anusan Market,** on the corner of Sri Dornchai and Chang Klan, has plenty of local Thai and Chinese food stalls that offer excellent inexpensive food, as do the **Saturday Market, Sunday Market,** and **Warowot Market.** Expect to spend from 10 to 30B per dish or item.

Between Chang Phueak Road and Hussadhisawee Road is a daytime wet market and prepared-food market. Though you probably won't be carrying back any raw meats or vegetables to your hotel, the prepared food area is very accommodating to tourists. There is a coffee shop as well as a sit-down area with pictures of the dishes offered. These visuals are perfect if your Thai isn't quite up to speed. Try one of the many Thai desserts or, if you're braver, one of the many varieties of crunchy insects. Another location that is worth checking out if you happen to be on your way to Doi Suthep or around Nimmanhemin Road is the food stalls surrounding Chiang Mai University.

Local Cuisine

Khao soi—soft noodles in sweet, savory rich yellow curry, covered with crispy fried noodles and usually served with chicken or beef—is one of Chiang Mai's best-known dishes. The provenance of the dish is not clear. Some maintain it is an interpretation of a Shan dish, others that it is a Thai Muslim dish, and others that it's a hybrid of both. Wherever it comes from, to really know Chiang Mai you'll have to try a dish yourself. Though nearly every restaurant serves it, you'll find the best renditions in an area locally referred to as **Fa Ham.** The neighborhood is on the east bank of the Ping River, across the Naowarat Bridge in the area surrounding Charoen Rat Road. Here you'll find a bunch of open-air *khao soi* restaurants, but **Kao Soi Lam Duan** (352/22 Fa Ham Rd., tel. 05/324-3519, 8 A.M.–4 P.M. daily, 40B) is considered by most to be the best in the neighborhood.

If you're not in the Kao Soi Lam Duan neighborhood, head for the nameless restaurant with the yellow sign reading **Kaow Soi** in English (Phra Pokklao Rd, across from Three Kings' Monument, tel. 08/5618-1041, 6 A.M.–3 P.M. daily, 30B). This is a very casual, local place serving *khao soi,* soups, and garlic rice, a great accompaniment to the traditional dish. This may not be the most beautiful restaurant in the city, but the *khao soi* is among the best.

Sa Nga Choeng Doi (no phone, 40B) is worth the adventure it takes to find it. From the northwest corner of the moat, head down Hussadhisawee Road (there is a little police box on the corner). About five blocks down, Chanoensuk Road on your left will be the first noticeable signage. Head down this street and on your left (across from the School of Massage for Health, Chiang Mai) you'll see the red-and-white tablecloths, which means you've arrived. With no roman script and a garagelike atmosphere, this place offers some of the best northern Thai and Muslim food in town. The *roti mataba* (curry in a roti shell) with the little cucumber salad and the *khao mok gai* are the

most popular and chances are you will be the only tourist in sight.

Directly across from the Royal Princess Hotel, **Den Duang Restaurant** (147/1 Chang Khlan Rd., tel. 05/327-5333, 10 A.M.–10 P.M. daily, 70B) has mostly Thai patrons. If it is delectable Thai food you are after, grab a seat and check out their comprehensive Thai menu, with meat and fish and seafood dishes besides just the normal tourist-friendly pad thai and stir fries. They have a few Western dishes as well (think spaghetti). The one thing you wouldn't expect from this Thai-oriented menu is their serious array of drinks—they have coffees, teas, and trendy cocktails.

Sailomjoy (7 Ratchadamnoen Rd., no phone, 7:30 A.M.–4 P.M. daily, 40B) is a popular spot for younger tourists and offers good, inexpensive Thai standards and some Western baked goods in the morning. This is a very casual spot; the big draws here are the inexpensive set breakfast, the fresh fruit juices and shakes, and the mango sticky rice.

For charming, lively atmosphere, head to the popular **Riverside Bar and Restaurant** (9–11 Charoenrat Rd., tel. 05/324-3239, www.theriversidechiangmai.com, 11 A.M.–1 A.M. daily, 250B). The large, well-established restaurant on the Ping River serves an expansive Thai menu of everything from pad thai to *khao soi,* but the darker curries here are particularly tasty, such as the Burmese and the Massaman, and the panang curry has a bite that can stay with you all evening. There are also burgers and pizza if your dining companions are looking for something a little more familiar, and vegetarian fare for non-meat eaters. There is also a nightly dinner cruise at 8 P.M.; make sure to make reservations if you want to dine on the water. After dinner the restaurant often has live music, and stays open till 1 A.M.

Just across from Nimanhemin Soi 1 is the **⟨ Hong Tauw Inn** (95/16–17 Nimmanhemin Rd., tel. 05/321-8333, 11 A.M.–midnight daily, 150B), which translates as "Shop House." Full of quirky decorations and funky clocks, this restaurant offers a wide range of classic Thai dishes. There are also quite a few set-menu options for two or four people, which is perfect if you're new to Thai food or if you like to share (sharing is Thai tradition; the formal northern meal in which food is shared and hands are used is called *khan toke*). The real winners include the green curry and the northern sausage, and don't be afraid to try the whole fish or a spicy salad. Another helpful feature of the menu is the phonetically written Thai coupled with English descriptions; this way you can order your favorites at a later date *and* practice your Thai.

Although **Aroon Rai** (Kotchasam Rd., Tha Phae Gate, tel. 05/327-6947, 9:30 A.M.–10 P.M. daily, 60B) often has a decent number of foreigners in attendance, this shouldn't take away from the absolute "Thainess" of the place. With very little ornamentation, this place is concerned with only the food. The *som tam* (spicy papaya salad), *khao soi,* and *gaeng hong lay* (a popular dark northern curry with pork) are all quite good. If you're feeling adventurous try the *rot duan* (caterpillar), *meng muan* (termite), or *ging gong* (cricket).

Fitting right into the Nimanhemin neighborhood, **Khun Nai Teun Sai** (Nimanhemin Soi 11, tel. 05/322-2208, 5:30 P.M.–midnight daily, 150B) is a casual but elegant place for dinner. The modern restaurant, decorated with modern art, offers well-prepared typical Thai dishes such as spring rolls and *satay,* but is more about atmosphere. This is a great place for couples or groups of adults; children may feel a little less comfortable.

Khrua Phet Doi Ngam (267/1 Mahidon Rd., tel. 05/320-4517, 11 A.M.–9 P.M. daily, 100B) is another adventure within itself. It is a ways out of the city towards the southwest; if you are traveling by taxi or *tuk tuk,* you can just show this to the driver: ครัวเพชรดอยงาม. They have authentic soups such as *kaeng pak siang da khai mot,* a vegetable curry with ant eggs. They also offer frog (*kop*) and a northern sausage, *sai ua.* Don't be afraid to ask the waiter what is good, or simply say *arai godai* (which basically means "whatever") and hope for the best.

Khan Toke
ขันโตก

Khan toke is a special Thai dinner indigenous to Chiang Mai, in which various dishes are served on a large tray, either made of teak (*yuan khan toke*) or woven bamboo and rattan (*Lao khan toke*). The presentation is lovely, but the real attraction is the variety of foods you'll get to sample. Your meal will be an assortment of dishes, including *namphrik* dips and curries, and sticky rice and/or plain rice, as well as dessert. There are many places in the city that offer this meal, some with a traditional dance show. A few worth visiting are **Old Chiang Mai Cultural Center** (185/3 Wualai Rd., tel. 05/320-2993, www.old chiangmai.com, 7–9:30 P.M. daily, 400B), **Antique House** (1 Charoen Prathet Rd., tel. 05/327-6810, 11 A.M.–midnight daily, 400B), and ◖ **Khum Khantoke** (139 Mu 4, Nong Pakrung, tel. 05/330-4121, 7–10 P.M. daily, 350B). All of these also have classical dance and music shows and nice settings in old teak houses. It's all a little touristy and contrived, but the performances are well executed and the food is good. Antique House also gets great reviews as a regular à la carte restaurant, but if you want to catch a show and have the full dinner at any of these places make sure to call ahead for reservations.

Vegetarian

Located on the inside of Tha Phae Gate, next to Black Canyon Coffee, **Aum Restaurant** (65 Moon Muang Rd., tel. 05/327-8315, 8 A.M.–2 P.M. and 5–9 P.M. daily, 50B) offers an extensive vegetarian menu that locals rave about. Also a great used bookshop, this charming spot captures the essence of Chiang Mai in one small hole-in-the-wall restaurant. The extremely tasty *khao soi* comes with tofu and potatoes instead of chicken or beef and there are plenty of other vegetarian options to choose from. The lack of sugar in the fruit shakes is well appreciated and if dragonfruit is an option, the color will not disappoint.

International Cuisine

A relatively new restaurant with a locally well-known Mediterranean chef, **Girasole** (71 Ratchadamnoen Rd., tel. 05/327-6388, www.lagondolathailand.com, 11 A.M.–11 P.M. daily, 300B) is most decidedly Italian, and not an Asian impersonation (except a baby corn in the soup here or there), and the food is downright delicious. They have a plethora of pasta dishes and a lot of different pastas to choose from including a spinach and spirulina fettucini that is enjoyable even if you're not super health conscious. Besides pizzas out of a brick oven (open for spectators), they also have meat and seafood dishes, and Italian appetizers as well such as minestrone soup and carpaccio. Don't forget to end with a gelato or something from their dessert menu. The service is very good, and even better if the kind manager/chef is there. It won't break your wallet, either; the prices are the same as any other Italian place around. The best time to go is for dinner, especially if you get a table in the courtyard.

Run by the same people as Girasole is an Italian fusion–inspired place called **Caffé Gourmet** (39/7–8 Ratchamankha Rd., tel. 05/328-3824, www.lagondolathailand.com, 11 A.M.–11 P.M. Tues.–Sun., 300B). Right in the middle of backpacker heaven, it is a swank place with jazz on Saturday nights.

For a quick bite drop into **Jerusalem Falafel** (35/3 Moon Muang Rd., tel. 05/327-0208, 9 A.M.–11 P.M. Sat.–Thurs., 80B). The tried-and-true place for Israeli food, this is the place to come if it is hummus or tabouleh that you are missing. Jerusalem Falafel also has a bakery and soups and baguettes.

Mike's (Tha Phae Gate, Chiyaphum Rd. and Anusan Market at the Night Bazaar, 6 P.M.–3 A.M. daily, 100B) has a loyal following among the local expat community and has been "converting vegetarians" since 1979 (depending when you arrive, it may seem more like they are "serving the drunk after-hours crowd"). Open until 3 A.M. and now with locations outside the city center, Mike's has burgers, chili dogs, and onion rings. Also milkshakes—malted, even. Their options also include chicken burgers and breakfast deals (bacon and eggs), chili, and garlic bread—sure to satisfy any nostalgia for American cuisine.

It may look like a bit of a tourist trap, but **Chiang Mai Saloon** (30 Radvitri Rd., tel. 05/321-9667, 10 A.M.–11 P.M. daily, 200B) has a real Tex-Mex menu complete with yummy, soft flour tortillas. This is a true down-home saloon, with writing covering the wooden tables and walls and beer specials. They even make their own refried beans. Besides Southwestern favorites, they have a separate Thai menu. There is a lively atmosphere in the evenings, with either sports on TV or live music.

Cafés

Since so much coffee is grown in the mountains of northern Thailand, it's not surprising that it seems like everyone in Chiang Mai is obsessed with coffee and café culture. In addition to large international chains (the largest Starbucks in the country is in Chiang Mai) and multiple **Black Canyon Coffee** outlets, there are plenty of smaller cafés brewing locally harvested coffee and tea and serving cakes and pastries.

◖ **Tea House Siam Celadon** (158 Tha Phae Rd., tel. 05/323-4518, 9:30 A.M.–6 P.M. daily, 100B) is in an elegant, renovated colonial-style building and serves tea, coffee, and light meals in an airy gorgeous but relaxed setting. You'll get to sample teas grown around the region, as well as sandwiches, pastas, and ice cream. If you find yourself coveting the plate your club sandwich is on, you can buy it. The teahouse is also a celadon shop and many of the pieces you see are for sale there.

Despite its prime location near the Tha Phae Gate, **Bake and Bite** (6/1 Kotchasarn Soi 1, tel. 05/328-5185, 7 A.M.–6 P.M. Mon.–Sat., 7 A.M.–3 P.M. Sun., 100B) manages to feel isolated and extremely peaceful. It's a great place to stop in for some excellent coffee and pastries if you're tired from sightseeing and shopping. If you're a little hungrier, there are sandwiches and salads too. There is also a location on Nimanhamen Soi 6.

Across the Naowarat Bridge, away from the old city just off Tha Phae Road, is **Love at First Bite** (28 Chiang Mai–Lamphun Soi 1, tel. 05/324-2731, 7 A.M.–4 P.M. daily, 100B). If you are in need of a few moments of peace and quiet and you have a sweet tooth, this is an ideal stop. The lush garden and glass enclosure allows air-con appreciators to also embrace the surroundings. The menu is extremely colorful and although it features desserts, it also has some hearty staples such as macaroni and cheese and chicken pot pie. Some particularly explosive choices include the volcano cheesecake and the love cup. There are also quite a few varieties of cheesecake, including a green-tea slice. With corny classical adaptations of Broadway musicals playing in the background, Love at First Bite is an ideal dessert destination.

GETTING THERE
Air
The **Chiang Mai International Airport** (60 Mahidal Rd., Suthep, tel. 05/327-0222, www2.airportthai.co.th, airport code: CNX), located 10 minutes southwest of Chiang Mai city, is a relatively small and quiet airport, but you can still expect all the usual modern conveniences of ATMs, foreign-exchange services, tour and taxi agents, and a few small shops and cafés. Recent air-route deregulation has lured a lot of budget carriers out this way, including **Nok Air** (www.nokair.com) and **Air Asia** (www.airasia.com), and the increased competition has reduced fares to the point that even budget travelers often abandon the more traditional overland routes. A one-way fare from Bangkok will typically set you back 1,500–2000B, but you can sometimes find one for as little as 600B. If you fly out of Bangkok check your tickets carefully; the majority of flights to Chiang Mai leave from the new Suvarnabhumi airport, but a handful still leave from Bangkok's older Don Muang airport. Daily domestic flights come and go on six airlines to most of the country's major airports, and a few international routes per week fly to nearby countries, although most travelers arriving from outside Thailand will be routed through Bangkok.

There is a taxi-service counter on the main floor where you can arrange a lift to the city;

the standard fare to most parts of the city is 120B. It's a good idea to check with your hotel before you arrive because many of them offer a free transfer service.

Train
Rumbling along on a cross-country train trip is probably the most flavorful way to get to Chiang Mai, especially if you haven't had the chance to ride the rails this way before. It's also one of the most economical, and unfortunately one of the slowest, options, taking up to 14 hours to complete and costing under 1,000B for a second-class overnight sleeper.

The Chiang Mai railway station (27 Charoen Muang Rd.) is the country's northernmost train station and is positioned just east of town on the far side of the Ping River; it's not much more than a platform, but there are a few kiosks selling drinks, snacks, maps, and souvenirs. Taxis and *tuk tuks* are usually waiting to take passengers into town; some hotels will also arrange a pickup for you.

Bus
Chiang Mai's two bus stations see dozens of coaches rolling in and out every day, providing fairly respectable access to south Thailand and to most northern towns. The Chiang Mai Arcade Bus Terminal (tel. 05/324-4664) is northeast of the city center and handles the Bangkok, Chiang Rai, and Pai routes; while the Chang Phueak Bus Terminal (tel. 05/321-1586) is just north of the Chang Phueak Gate and services the majority of the other routes.

Car
With the white-knuckle insanity of Bangkok traffic, it's surprising that so many visitors to the kingdom opt to rent a car in the capital for their trip to Chiang Mai, but in reality it's a fairly popular option. Of course if you want to really experience the trek north, with the freedom to explore whatever captures your interest, it's definitely your best choice, and once you're outside of the urban area the drive becomes rather pleasant and

the roads are well marked. In the eight-hour drive from Bangkok you are bound to see a lot of Thailand, much of it beautiful and fascinating, and there are a number of interesting spots where you can stop along the way. There are two possible routes for this trip; the first is to take Highway 1 (Phahonyothin Road) and then turn onto Highway 32 (Asia Highway), passing Ayutthaya, Angthong, and Nakhon Sawan, then switch to Highway 117 until Phitsanulok, and finally Highway 11 from Lampang to Chiang Mai. Alternatively you can stay on Highway 1 from Nakhon Sawan, passing Kamphaeng Phet, Tak, and Lampang, to Chiang Mai. They both take about the same amount of time, so choose based on what you want to see along the way.

GETTING AROUND

The old city, within the bounds of the moat, is less than three square kilometers in area, making it easily walkable if you want to explore the *wats* and markets on foot. Depending on where you are in relation to the Tha Phae Gate, it's also an easy walk to the Night Market just east of the old city. If you're heading very far outside of the old city, to the Nimmanhemin area for example, you'll probably need to use motorized transport. Just outside of the moat is a multilane roadway that circles the old city, with fast-moving cars and motorbikes at nearly all hours of the day. Once you cross that road, traffic slows down again and is more manageable.

Bicycles

Many guesthouses and resorts have bikes available for rental by the day and this can be a nice way to get around. Chiang Mai is a big city, however, and even inside the moat area there are plenty of cars and motorbikes, making it difficult to cross streets or even change lanes with a slow-moving bicycle. Only those who are confident on two wheels find biking beyond the moat pleasant.

Motorbikes

There are a handful of rental shops in the old

city and on the road surrounding the moat renting motorbikes and scooters by the day. Rates vary but expect to pay between 200 and 300B per day. Many guesthouses and hotels also offer scooter rental or can arrange to have a bike brought to you; make sure to ask as you may be able to avoid an unnecessary trip.

Song Thaew

These modified pickup trucks with two benches in the back are very popular in Chiang Mai and offer a convenient, inexpensive, and slightly adventurous means of getting around. They run from around 7 A.M. to 7 P.M. depending on the route; many of the trucks running routes heading out of the city stop and start at Warowat Market and are color coded. If you're going somewhere within the city (even if outside of the old city), you'll probably be taking one of the ubiquitous red *song thaew,* which run on fixed routes and can also be used as taxis if there are no other passengers. Typically you stand on the sidewalk and flag one down; some of the fixed-route *song thaew* have signs in English indicating where they are going. Tell the driver where you're going and he'll let you know if he's going there or not, then you clamber up into the back and you're on your way. When you want to get off, press the button on the bars above you and he'll pull over, then go around to his window and pay him (maximum 15B inside town unless he takes you to a custom destination).

Though *song thaew* are not allowed to pick up at the airport, they can take you there when you are departing from the city. Expect to pay less than 100B regardless of the number of passengers.

Though there is no posted schedule in English for *song thaew,* most every resident of the city will know the schedules and general routes, so do not be afraid to ask where you can pick one up to take you wherever you are going.

Tuk Tuks

Tuk Tuks are available throughout the city and travel both to city destinations and places a few kilometers out of the city. Fares are entirely up to negotiation, but expect to pay between 20B and 60B for a short ride.

Samlor

Chiang Mai is one of the few cities in the country where rickshaw-like bicycles still ply the streets. It's not the fastest way to get around, and you can't fit more than a couple of people and a few bags into one of the *samlor,* but they tend to be popular with visitors anyway. *Samlor* are generally slightly more expensive than *tuk tuks* and are also subject to negotiation with the driver. Though you'll see them all over the city, many *samlor* drivers congregate around the Warowat Market during the day.

samlor driver in Chiang Mai

© SUZANNE NAM

Excursions from Chiang Mai

For many travelers the real appeal of a visit to Chiang Mai lies in the greater Chiang Mai Province or just beyond, outside of the city. If you like adventure or are athletically inclined, you will probably find yourself among this group. Apart from the obvious jungle trekking and hiking, there is an impressive selection of outdoor activities available through local tour agencies and guesthouses, including the regular complement of mountain biking and horseback riding as well as some more exotic options such as bungee-jumping and even glider rentals. However if that's not your idea of a good time you can explore craft villages, visit with the hill tribe people, lose yourself in flower gardens, brave the snake farms, and take in the Chiang Mai Zoo or one of the famous elephant camps. Chiang Mai is a day-tripper's paradise and unless you've got a lot of time it's likely that you won't get a chance to do it all; it's a good idea to short-list some of the things that you really don't want to miss.

Tour Operators

If you're planning on making a trip to one of the outlying villages, there are plenty of tour companies in the city of Chiang Mai who can set up either a group or individual tour and many people schedule hiking and other tours (even multiday tours involving camping) as little as one day before they'd like to depart. Many guesthouses function as tour sales agents or even lead tours themselves, so it's not necessary to worry too much about planning ahead here. Though there are scores of tour agencies, the tours themselves are usually quite similar to one another and the tours on offer include day tours to Doi Suthep, Doi Intha Non, the Handicraft Highway, and elephant camps. Multiday hiking tours will almost always be group tours and are structured to include a visit to an elephant camp, hiking, bamboo rafting on a river, and accommodations in a hill tribe village. Though it may feel a little canned, it is a great way to see many things the region has to offer conveniently and with a guide. If you want something different, you'll need to negotiate that in advance and expect to pay substantially more if you're asking a guide to get off the well-beaten path.

Because there is often a middle man involved in selling these excursions, prices are subject to negotiation and sometimes travelers will find that they paid more or less than other travelers for the same trip. If you are on a budget, shop around and compare prices before spending your baht.

WAT PHRA THAT DOI SUTHEP
วัดพระธาตุดอยสุเทพ

Possibly the most renowned *wat* in Chiang Mai and an important footprint of the Lanna Kingdom, the 600-hundred-year-old mountaintop monastery **Wat Phra That Doi Suthep** (Huay Kaew Rd., 6 A.M.–8 P.M. daily, 50B with tram ride, 30B without) has a number of features that make it worth the 16-kilometer journey outside of the city, and this half-day excursion is a must for any visitor to Chiang Mai. A prime example of the lavish grandeur of the Lanna Kingdom, Doi Suthep remains one of the holiest sites in the kingdom and is a major pilgrimage site for faithful Buddhists. Even if you take the trip only for the stunning view you will be rewarded with a postcard vista of Chiang Mai city, especially at sunrise and sunset. If the view alone is not enough to draw you, there is still the mysterious Buddha relic, with its reputation for performing miracles, buried beneath the pagoda, and the many free daily programs offered by the International Buddhism Center housed there. Try to visit on a weekday—the weekend crowds can be oppressive—and if at all possible in time for sunrise or sunset when the view is at its most exhilarating.

Once you get to the temple, have a look at the giant *nagas* that line the sides of the stairs, and as you ascend keep a sharp eye out for some of the tropical birds that live on the mountain. Once at the top, pause outside the walls to check out the many temple bells. Don't be shy about ringing them (softly) for good luck. You will also find a small snack bar to refresh you after the hike. At the back of the outer area is a small museum and a good spot to take in the view of Chiang Mai. As soon as you enter the inner compound you will notice the giant gold-colored Lanna-style *chedi* that houses the

Buddha relic; the four elaborate umbrellas that surround the *chedi* are also interesting. Don't forget to head around the back of the compound where the most impressive *wiharn* (outbuilding containing images of Lord Buddha) sits. You will see a number of Buddha images around the compound, but the white marble Buddha near this *wiharn* stands apart from those made of more common materials. As you wander through the complex, watch among the usual images and statuary for the unique and strangely lifelike monks cast in metal, gaze at the abundant murals with vibrant depictions of Buddha's life, and wonder at the strange rituals of merit-making that you will see all around you. Beyond just the typical sticks of incense and lotus flowers, you will see flags tied to bodhi trees, gold leaf scratched onto many surfaces, flags made of currency notes, and even coins pressed into tablets of wax. There is also a beautiful museum building with a small collection of Buddhas and Thai currency.

According to legend, the relic lurking beneath the pagoda is a shoulder bone from Buddha himself (*phra that* means relic of the Buddha), found after an old priest had a dream telling him where to look for it. Once dug up the relic reportedly performed occasional miracles, such as glowing brightly with a mysterious internal light, and at one point even replicating itself. The priest later came to Lanna to teach Buddhism, bringing the bone with him, and after it spontaneously doubled plans were made to build a pagoda in honor of the powerful relic. The only trouble was finding the right place for the tribute, and so an appropriately elaborate scheme was devised. The relic was put on the back of a white elephant who was then turned loose to roam about at will, the idea being that wherever the elephant decided to stop to rest was where the pagoda would be built. The elephant headed up the hill, passing up very convenient locations for construction along the way, and eventually stopped way up the mountainside at the *wat*'s current location. The elephant died shortly thereafter and a monument still stands on the temple grounds to honor his contribution; you can see it standing along the wall at the corner to your left from the top of the stairs.

Before you make your way back down to earth, you might want to spend a few moments in the bookstore where you can find English literature on Buddhism and a selection of Thai and northern Thai music. If you have questions or are interested in learning more about Buddhism, you can visit the International Buddhist Center and talk to one of the monks who can answer all your questions, and in English no less. At the center you can also find out about the courses and programs that they offer.

Getting There

To get to the mountain, you can take a red *song thaew* from Chiang Mai University, Chang Phueak Gate, or Chiang Mai Zoo for around 100B round-trip (or flag one down anywhere along the route). These run multiple times an hour during the day. From the parking area at the base of Doi Suthep mountain you can enjoy the leisurely tram ride up to Wat Phra That Doi Suthep, or you can brave the 309 steps that will take you to where the temple sits halfway up the mountain.

THE RUINS OF WIANG KUM KAM
เวียงกุมกาม

For an interesting cultural half-day trip from Chiang Mai, consider the ruins of the town of Wiang Kum Kam, located between the Ping River and Lamphun highway. This city was originally a Mon settlement and existed as a satellite in the Haripujaya Kingdom based in Lamphun until the 12th century. It then was claimed by the Lannathai when they toppled the Mon Empire; it's believed that King Mengrai lived here for a few years before Chiang Mai was built. Abandoned for 300 years because of flooding, Wiang Kum Kam became a town in legend only until it was rediscovered in 1984 after local people found a number of artifacts in the area. Rumors of valuable relics began to circulate, attracting would-be treasure

hunters, and the Fine Arts Department finally stepped in to preserve the site. There are now 42 historical monuments spread over the nine-square-kilometer site; most are simply ruined platforms and *chedi,* but there are two *wats* still in operation and the peaceful country scenery is enjoyable in itself. Start out at **Wat Chedi Liam** (วัดเจดีย์เหลี่ยม), or Wiang Kum Kam (วัดกู่คำหลวง, where you will find an information center orienting you to the site and describing the historical significance of the town and the lifestyle of the people who lived there. You can also see a good example of Lanna architecture if you look at the *wat*'s main assembly hall, which was built entirely without nails. Since Wiang Kum Kam is too big to cover on foot, you can also rent a bicycle, hire a pony carriage, or join a tour around the site from this *wat*. The other still-functioning temple, **Wat Kan Thom** (วัดกานโถม), or Wat Chang Kham (วัดช้างคำ), is the more attractive of the two and some believe that King Mengrai's spirit still resides there today. Khan Tom also has a Cultural and Local Wisdom Learning Center where you can see a replica of a traditional Lanna house and other objects. There is also a Lanna market selling food and local clothing, though it's really a re-creation for tourists and not authentic.

Getting There

There is no regular bus or *song thaew* service out to Wiang Kum Kam (เวียงกุมกาม), so you'll either need to hire a ride for the ten-kilometer trip or make the drive yourself. If hiring a ride, you'll have to negotiate with the driver, but expect to pay about 100B if you are going one way. It might be a good idea to have the driver wait, though, since you may not find a ride back easily. If driving, take Route 106 (Chiang Mai–Lamphun Rd.) south for five kilometers and look for the Wiang Kum Kam sign, which is in Thai: เวียงกุมกาม. From here it's a further two kilometers until the right turn into the park. Alternatively veer right onto Ko Klang Road (just after the Holiday Inn) from Route 106 and head south, hugging the river for about half a kilometer before turning right into the park; this will put you on the road to Wat Chedi Liam.

CHIANG MAI ZOO
สวนสัตว์เชียงใหม่

The Chiang Mai Zoo (100 Huay Kaew Rd., tel. 05/322-1179, admin@chiangmaizoo.com, 8 A.M.–9 P.M. daily, 50B adult, 30B child), renovated in 2004, is an excellent zoo. In fact its 7,000 avian, reptilian, and mammalian residents enjoy over 80 hectares of cleverly designed, spacious habitat with such rich flora and inconspicuous barriers that it's possible to occasionally forget that you're in a zoo at all. Positioned at the foot of Doi Suthep, the facility has been around since 1974 but was fairly unremarkable until 2004 when a pair of black-and-white new arrivals sparked enough "panda-monium" to attract a huge injection of cash, which funded the spiffy layout you see today. The beautifully landscaped grounds are spacious and green, and infusions of tropical flowers and restaurants with great views of Chiang Mai city beckon visitors, offering a tranquil setting for their animal adventures. In a way it's the park's funky design even more than its animal collection that makes it worth a visit—there are only a handful of species here that stand out from the usual menagerie of other large zoos, but here you can see them in a whole new way. Unique features making this a fun day out include paths through wide-open forested compounds where different animals run about freely together; raised walkways and platforms aimed at setting up unique vantage points for viewing the animals and their environment; and a few opportunities to get closer to the inmates than most animal parks will allow.

The animals tend to be more restful during midday, so if possible start out early so you can see them going about their morning activities, and in some cases munching on their breakfasts. Once you're ready to start exploring, take a moment to look at the big map near the entrance and plan which displays you really want to take in so that you don't end up backtracking in the mazelike zoo. There's a lot to see but

try to include the white tiger and of course the star attraction, the much-loved giant pandas. The zoo is arranged around a very long loop road with smaller trails leading off to and from the different exhibit areas; you'll find food and drink kiosks along with washrooms throughout the park, so once you know what you want to see you are ready to start exploring. The biggest attractions are listed below, roughly in order from the northern part of the zoo (near the Huay Kaew Rd. entrance, on the road to Doi Suthep), to the southern part.

Nakornping Aviary

With about one hectare of rambling forest and 800 free-flying inhabitants, the Nakornping Aviary is one attraction definitely worth a visit. As you walk along the shady green forest floor, searching for the feathered denizens and enjoying the flowers, one thing you won't notice is the enclosing netting cleverly concealed high above the treetops so as not to break the mood. Perhaps the most interesting aspect of the aviary, though, is the walkways that ascend upward through the trees, taking you all the way to leaf-level where you can get a unique "bird's-eye" perspective on life in the jungle canopy.

Open Zoo

Another open-concept exhibit is the "Open Zoo" area that is home to over 200 peacefully mingling critters, including the zoo's collection of deer. Raised walkways through this 16-hectare enclosure keep you on track and aid you in getting a good view of the wildlife. From time to time you can also find vendors selling snacks so that you can try out hand-feeding some of the animals; the giraffes are especially gracious diners.

Freshwater Aquarium

If you've gazed into the murky waters of one of Thailand's many rivers and wondered what might be lurking beneath, or if you engage in the occasional angling trip back home, then you might want to check out the zoo's freshwater aquarium, just west of the aviary. Featuring 60 species of Southeast Asia's tropical freshwater fish, there are some rather rare and impressive varieties on display, including the giant Mekong catfish, the Siamese giant carp, and the ture eel.

Giant Pandas

The zoo's beloved pair of giant pandas were presented to the Thai government as "friend-ship ambassadors" by the government of China in 2004 in honor of Queen Sirikit's birthday in 2004; they were placed in the care of the Zoological Park Organization of Thailand, who chose the Chiang Mai Zoo as their home. Because there are so few opportunities to see giant pandas outside of China, the gift instantly put Chiang Mai's zoo on the map, drawing thousands of Thais and foreigners every year who line up for a chance to peek at the rare and elusive giants. Unfortunately the park makes good use of these undeniably cute celebrities, charging an extra 100B (50B for kids) for entrance into their fancy state-of-the-art (and delightfully air-conditioned) compound to see them, but most people figure it's worth it. The pandas get their breakfast at 9 A.M. and are usually pretty active at this time of day; if you turn up in the afternoon you're less likely to see panda antics, but then they're still pretty adorable even when they're just relaxing. Just like other celebrities, Lin Hui and Chuang Chuang have had a tough time keeping their sex life (or lack of it) out of the news, and the zoo's burning desire to see a few baby pandas tumbling onto the scene has led to a few strange escapades that were picked up by MSNBC and others. Chuang Chuang has been placed on a slimming diet to improve his sex appeal, but earlier attempts to set the mood by staging a wedding for the pair, and bringing in some steamy panda mating videos for them to enjoy together, have failed to produce results. The couple is scheduled to return to China in 2013, so the keepers still have time to give oysters and chocolate a try.

Children's Zoo

Naturally the zoo is an ideal spot to visit if you're counting any kids among your traveling companions. Apart from the usual appeal of animals, open spaces, and sunshine, the park also has a separate area designated as the Children's Zoo. This section is a big grassy area up on top of a small hill in the southern part of the zoo, were you'll find several playgrounds along with a bunch of kid-friendly games and exhibits. They can also get a bit of hands-on time with some of the animals at the smallish petting zoo, and occasionally donkey rides are available.

Getting There and Around

The zoo is located at the base of Doi Suthep, right after Chiang Mai University on Huay Kaew Road. A short *tuk tuk* ride (about 100B) will get you to the zoo from the city center or if you like, any of the *song thaew* headed for Wat Doi Suthep can also drop you at the entrance to the park. You can find these *song thaew* at Chang Phueak Gate (referred to as Pratu) on the north edge of the old city but if you're already on the main road you can either flag one down or board at Chiang Mai University. You'll have no trouble picking one up in the return direction because there are always a few drivers hanging around the exit waiting for a fare. The park's huge grounds and hillside location mean that if you decide to go on foot you're in for a lot of walking, much of it uphill; but if that turns you off then take one of the open-air trams running between exhibits (20B for an all-day tram ticket), or you can even take your rental vehicle in with you (30B per car, 10B per motorcycle).

BAN THAWAI
บานถวาย

Dedicated shoppers should consider making the short trip to Ban Thawai (90 Mu 2 Ban Thawai, Khun Khong, Hang Dong, tel. 08/1882-4882, www.ban-tawai.com, 9 A.M.–5:30 P.M. daily), a small village 16 kilometers outside of town off of Hang Dong Road to the south. Sponsored by OTOP (One Tambon One Product—a government program designed to encourage villages to make and sell handicrafts), Ban Thawai is akin to an outlet center for any kind of specialty

Thai art. Everything is sold wholesale, and you can't beat the prices—if you have already spent time around the Sunday Market in town, you will notice the difference. Ban Thawai is mainly known as a woodcarving village, but now it is also a center for traditional rattan work, bamboo goods and crafts, furniture, lamps, pottery, and all sorts of other artwork and handicrafts. It supports a traditional industry by bringing hand-made original goods to consumers. There is a lot of original design and styles—you will see many "no photos please" signs. The sheer number of places and amount of handmade goods is astonishing. The quality is very good all around; you may find items to be more "polished" at the more upscale showrooms and boutiques in Ban Thawai, although the prices will reflect this.

Allow yourself a trip here to gaze around, and then to buy. The village and different "zones" are very well marked, which makes it only slightly less overwhelming.

Many visitors, Thai and foreign alike, come with the purpose to buy furniture or large-scale items. Rest assured, most places are equipped for shipping.

Getting There

The best way to get to Ban Thawai if you're not driving yourself is to hire a taxi or *tuk tuk* for a few hours (expect to pay a few hundred baht for the round trip). You'll probably need the space to carry everything you've bought, and on the way to Ban Thawai there are many producers, manufacturers, and exporters of wooden goods and locally made crafts—though you'll really want to check out Ban Thawai before buying anything else.

BO SANG AND SAN KAMPHAENG
บอสรางและสันกำแพง

Every year thousands of faithful shoppers make a pilgrimage to the handicrafts mecca that is San Kamphaeng Road, aka the **Handicrafts Highway,** which, along with the charming Umbrella Village of Bo Sang, makes up a little shopping district where you can peruse some surprisingly unique goods and get a first-hand look at how these traditional arts are created. Along this stretch of highway there is also a hot springs and a sacred cave to add a little variety to your day trip; you should plan to spend four hours to a whole day out here.

Bo Sang
บอสราง

Bo Sang is located eight kilometers east of Chiang Mai on Route 1006; once there you will quickly see that the title of Umbrella Village was not randomly assigned to this little community whose inhabitants specialize in the manufacture of natural papers and crafts made from the paper. *Sa* paper is made from the bark of the *sa* tree, which is native to the region and is a relative of the mulberry. Its use in paper-making has been understood and practiced by locals for many generations. The families of this town have been dedicated to the art of making parasols for over 200 years and have long been famous for their delicate and colorful creations. The process that begins with some tree bark and sticks of bamboo and ends with a filmy hand-painted parasol is a fascinating example of a traditional handicraft, and at Bo Sang you are able to view each step of the process. Historically, families would each have a particular specialty, with one making and cutting the paper, one constructing the frame, another putting them together, and the final family hand-painting them with traditional images. The easiest way to see the whole process from bark to bumbershoot is to visit either the **Umbrella Making Center** (corner of H1006 & R1014, tel. 05/333-8324, 8 A.M.–5 P.M.) or **The Sa Paper and Umbrella Handicraft Center** on Km 8 of H1006 (99/16 Baan Nongkong, San Kamphaeng Rd., tel. 05/333-8414, 8 A.M.–5 P.M.).

Bo Sang parasols have won awards for being one of the best travel souvenirs available worldwide, and the only trouble with taking one home with you will be choosing from the hundreds of designs available in sizes ranging from four inches to two meters across. Another fun option is to ask the local painters to paint a traditional Bo Sa design on a piece of clothing, on your bag, or on just about anything else that you want, though you will need to provide them with the item to be painted. You can have them paint any design you want from the usual floral subject matter to a 100 percent custom image of your own creation.

In late January Bo Sang puts on its annual **Umbrella Festival;** if you are in Chiang Mai at the time you should not miss it. The whole town is dolled up from head to toe with these umbrellas in a remarkable feat of color. There is an exotic procession in the streets featuring traditional costume and of course a lot of umbrellas, and every effort is made to keep the decor and events as close as possible to a traditional Lannathai festival.

San Kamphaeng
สันกำแพง

San Kamphaeng is a crafts village located just five kilometers further east of Bo Sang on Route 1006 and is traditionally famous for its pottery. Works from the kilns of Kamphaeng were highly regarded and sought after by the people of the Lanna Kingdom, and many of the antiques that you will see in the museums, temples, and antiques shops were crafted here. Nowadays however there is a lot more for sale than just ceramics and you will be able to find silver, antiques, silks, and wood products being sold alongside signature Lanna pottery products. The town's main street, San Kamphaeng Road, is a virtual gauntlet of shops not only fronted by the sidewalk, but spilling out onto it, and it is a major stop for tour buses, so arrive prepared to brave a crowd.

Muang On Cave
ถ้ำเมืองออน

San Kamphaeng is an easy jumping-off point for the spooky and mysterious Muang On Cave site and the privately owned San Kamphaeng Hot Springs, which lie about 19 kilometers east of town on Route 1317 and can be a much-needed diversion from the crowded shops and markets. Muang On Cave scores top points for atmosphere and is not for the faint of heart or the claustrophobic,

but it has a few features that make the trip from Chiang Mai more than worth the effort. From the car park you climb a 90-meter *naga* staircase to the cave's entrance. There you will find a small whitewashed *chedi,* built to house the earthly remains of the monk Phrakhru Ba Si Wichai, who spent much of his time meditating at the site, and whose ghost some claim to have seen in the cave. At the entrance you pay the attendants the 10B fee, which is used for maintenance of the site, and head downward into the gloomy heart of the cavern.

About a dozen steps or so down the concrete stairs that lead into the vault you have to stoop to squeeze through a narrow passageway for a short distance before continuing downward on the other side. Once through the passage electric fixtures light your way; stop frequently to look at the interesting features around you such as the wear patterns on the walls, the embedded minerals, and the occasional stalactite. As you continue downward keep your eye open for Buddhist icons occasionally tucked into the niches and natural ledges of the walls, including images of old men and a strange statue of a man with a cow's head. Further down you will come to a very strange site and one that is the subject of some controversy. Announced only by a small and unimpressive sign is the large and very impressive imprint of a prehistoric monster, which some claim is what's left of a dinosaur skeleton embedded in the 245 million-year-old cave wall. Although the validity of that claim remains untested, a careful look of the image is enough to spark debate. Creating an incredibly eerie effect, the nine-meter-long Phra Garoona Sai Yars reclining Buddha reposes languidly beneath the looming monster.

The stairs lead ultimately into a large open grotto that clearly shows the religious importance of the site to local Buddhists; strewn about in the niches and ledges of the cavern are Buddha images of all shapes and sizes left by followers who clearly felt a sense of spiritual awe in the presence of this incredible cavern. Presiding over the assembly is a large Buddha statue sitting high atop a natural ledge that perches above a natural basin of water. And just in case this isn't exactly your first cave and you're not easily impressed, the vault's centerpiece, the multihued nine-meter-tall and three-meter-wide **Jedee Mae Nomm Fah stalagmite** should be enough to tip the scales.

After the cavern—or instead, if the idea of descending into the bowels of the earth leaves you a feeling a little green—you can take a path leading from the cave's entrance and going further on up the hill where you can take in a Buddhist shrine and catch some really idyllic photos of Muang On Town and the valley below.

San Kamphaeng Hot Springs
น้ำพุร้อนสันกำแพง

One more kilometer east on Route 1317 is the turnoff (indicated by a large blue sign) for the hot springs; three kilometers down a small road are the relaxing San Kamphaeng Hot Springs (10B) and adjacent **Roong Aroon Resort** (108 Mu 7, Baan Sahakorn, Mae-On, tel. 05/324-8475, 20B to enter the springs). Here you will find natural geysers and steaming therapeutic mineral baths whose high sulfur content will quickly blacken your silver, so consider leaving your jewelry at the water's edge with your clothing! You can have a soak, take advantage of the handful of spa facilities that have sprung up, or stroll through the gardens nearby; both the San Kamphaeng Hot Springs and the Roong Aroon Resort offer accommodation if you take a liking to the spot.

Getting There

You have a few options for getting out to Bo Sang and San Kamphaeng. There are many daily buses that ply the route leaving Chiang Mai from Charoen Muang Road across from San Pa Khoi market; you can get off at Bo Sang or stay on until San Kampaeng. There are also *song thaew* leaving frequently from Chang Phueak bus terminal that will drop you at either location; both of these options will cost around 10B. Bo Sang is only nine kilometers from Chiang Mai, and San Kamphaeng is about 16 kilometers, so you don't have to worry about sweating it out on less-than-five-star local transportation for ages, making this option reasonable if you want the experience and if you aren't planning to pack a lot of new acquisitions back with you. A good way to do the trip is to rent a motorcycle or scooter in Chiang Mai to do the route, which gives you a lot more freedom of movement for as cheap as 200B per vehicle, and is probably the option that is the most fun. However if you are expecting to do a fair amount of shopping, renting a car or hiring a taxi for the day is next to essential for convenience and comfort, and can be arranged at one of many agents in Chiang Mai, or you can try to negotiate with a taxi driver on the street. You shouldn't have to pay more than 500B for the taxi service unless you are planning to travel further than San Kamphaeng, but as always ask around and see what price you can get. Alternatively many of the tour agencies will be offering this route as part of an organized day trip, which can be a fun and easy option.

DOI INTHANON
ดอยอินทนนท์

At 2,565 meters above sea level the cool, misty summit of Doi Inthanon is the highest point in all of Thailand, presiding over one of Chiang Mai Province's most popular national parks. Thick forest clings protectively to bogs, valleys, and hillsides, and shelters more than 350 species of tropical birds, as well as Hmong and Karen hill tribe settlements. It is a 97-kilometer excursion to the top of Doi Inthanon from Chiang Mai west along Highway 108, which has a smattering of artisan villages, dramatic mountain vistas, and waterfalls to break up the drive, but the round-trip can be done in a day if you start out early enough. This day trip is a good one to do by organized tour because they will ferry you to all of the best spots and you can sit back and enjoy the route's gorgeous scenery without worrying about navigating winding mountain passes and hairpin turns with steep vertical sides. If you do strike out on your own, it's best to skip the automatic motorcycles and scooters because they may struggle getting up some of the hills. Whatever you do, be sure to bring a jacket—the temperature at the top can be as low as 0 degrees Celsius during the winter when the humidity is high.

Mueang Kung Earthenware Village
บ้านเหมืองกุง

The first point of interest along the way is about 10 kilometers from town on Route 108. The Mueang Kung Earthenware Village, as the name suggests, is home to many artisans who specialize in pottery and earthenware in all shapes and styles, from traditional Lanna designs to more modern pieces. If you visit during the day you'll be able to find people working and even pick up some souvenirs. A few kilometers further on near the town of Hang Dong is the world-famous **Ban Thawai Woodcarving Village,** where purchasers come from all over the globe to buy home-decor pieces that will sell for many times the local price at shops in North America and Europe. This village is considered by many to be the cream of the crop in curio shopping in Thailand for price and quality, and it is a reservoir of traditional artistry where ancestral methods are preserved and employed in the creation of carved pieces in Lanna, Burmese, and even Tibetan styles. It's a great place to look for elegant gifts and eye-catching woodworks for your home.

Chom Thong
จอมทอง

The next stop is Chom Thong Town, at Km 58 on Route 108, where you can stop for some refreshment and to collect your energy before heading into the national park; it also claims what some believe to be the most beautiful temple in northern Thailand, **Wat Phra That Si Chom Thong,** for which Chom Thong District is named. The site dates back to the 14th century, although the current *wiharn* was built in 1817, and as you approach you are presented with an exquisite example of Lanna-Burmese woodcarving in the wonderfully rich gilt portico. Part of the beauty of this building is the wonderful flow of the design. Far from being stark and out of place, the carvings on

the outside fit perfectly with the interior and its beautiful Burmese-style altar and bronze Buddha images. Legend has it that part of the Buddha's skull was found on this spot in 749 and that it is still enshrined at the altar in this *wiharn,* for once residing aboveground rather than buried underneath a *chedi* as per the usual custom for Buddha relics. Before you leave stop to look at the delicately carved elephant tusks and the glass case near the altar that holds an interesting assortment of ancient Thai weaponry. The Burmese-style *chedi* near the *wiharn* is the oldest part of the temple and was part of the original construction in 1451.

Ban Rai Phai Ngam Cotton Weaving Village
บ้านไร่ผางาม

At this point you could continue 16 kilometers further south on Route 108 to visit the Ban Rai Phai Ngam Cotton Weaving Village, where the villagers weave cotton cloth in the old style with traditional looms. The **Pa Da Cotton Textile Museum** and associated textile factory (108 Chiang Mai–Hod Rd., tel. 05/336-1231, 8:30 A.M.–5 P.M. daily, factory closed on Thurs.), located in an old teak house, offers some well-done textile weaving displays. The left turnoff is just after Km 68; a three-kilometer road will take you to the village.

Doi Inthanon National Park
อุทยานแห่งชาติดอยอินทนนท์

You can head straight down the road to Doi Inthanon National Park (19 Ban-Luang Chom Thong, tel. 05/326-8550, 200B), which you passed just as you were heading into Chom Thong. From the north end of town, turn west onto Route 1009, which will take you past the toll booth where you can pay your 200B entry fee and get a brochure, and then through the park leading up to the summit.

The park covers 482 square kilometers of forest and includes the whole of Doi Inthanon mountain. As you travel toward the peak watch for the terraced rice fields of the hill tribes along its slopes, which make a great photo set among the misty greenery. This park is on the shortlist for naturalists who visit Thailand, and if you are very lucky you may spot some rare and exotic animals including swinging gibbons, the Indian civet, barking deer, giant flying squirrels, and the Asiatic black bear that counts this mountain as one of its last remaining habitats. There are numerous dirt tracks branching off from the main road, which lead to walking paths, meditation and prayer sanctuaries, and hill tribe villages, caves, and waterfalls. The smaller ones should not be attempted without four-wheel drive, especially during the rainy season. The first important spot to check out is the **Mae Ya waterfalls,** which crash to the earth in a tiered cascade from over 300 meters above. Another popular waterfall is the **Mae Klang Waterfalls.** You can drive most of the way to the falls, but you'll need to leave the car near the Buddhist College. After you park, cross the bridge leading to the gardens of the college and walk along a short footpath to the base of the falls. Nearby is **Birichinda Cave,** where you can see some remarkable stalagmites and stalactites along with an interior stream. It's worth stopping to walk around and take in the **Vachiratararn Falls,** one of the finest in the route's collection. You can stay in the bungalows here if you book ahead, or inquire about camping.

The summit of Doi Inthanon is misty, mossy, and comfortably flat; check out the visitors center for information on the ecology of the park, and look for the *chedi* above the center that holds the remains of Chao Inthawichayanon, the last ruler of the Lanna Kingdom before it merged with Siam. Most people get there by car using the 48-kilometer Summit Road in the park, however there is one trail that will take you to the top on foot. From the base the hike will take a moderately fit hiker around four hours. There is also a trail halfway up the summit, called Kew Mae Pan (at Km 42, the trail is closed June–Oct.). This is a beautiful though somewhat strenuous three-kilometer trail and is a good option for those who do not want to spend the whole day hiking but prefer not to drive all the way to the top. Moderately fit hikers can complete the trail in around two hours. There are a few walking paths at the summit, but most of them are restricted to reduce the impact on local plants and animals; across the road from the visitors center, however, the unrestricted Aangka Trail follows a boardwalk through a small sphagnum bog that is worth a look; wildlife is frequently spotted along this trail.

◖ THE MAE SA LOOP

Another option for a day trip from Chiang Mai is to wind your way along the scenic Mae Sa Loop (sometimes called the Samoeng Loop), following Routes 1096, 1269, and 107 into the beautiful Mae Sa Valley where you will find quiet roads, breathtaking scenery, and some rather well-done attractions to spice up the drive. You could conceivably spend two or three days seeing everything there is to see on this route, and accommodation is available at Samoeng and Mae Rim towns, as well as at various spots along Mae Rim–Samoeng Road, but one full day is enough to experience the best stuff. This strip of highway comes complete with world-class gardens, elephant camps, monkey training schools, doggie talent shows, snake farms, pony rides for kids, and a variety of ATV tours and bungee-jumping centers, to name a few of the options.

There are organized tours doing this loop, but you might have more fun renting a car or motorcycle and setting your own pace, especially because this route is considered one of the most scenic circuits in northern Thailand. Although public buses are available, they are infrequent and aren't a very realistic option for this stretch of highway. If you plan on driving you have to decide whether to head north toward the town of Mae Rim and then loop back around west and south to get home; or to leave Chiang Mai from the southeast and travel north to Samoeng, looping around east and back south on the return. Either way you'll have about 56 kilometers and a lot of stops to cover, especially if you take your camera. There are a number of picture-perfect viewpoints along the way and parts of the trip are very secluded and luxuriant. Give yourself at least a full day so that you can get the most out of it; you can also do it in two or more days by staying overnight in Mae Rim. There are some very windy stretches and in parts steep ravines next to the road, so if you decide to do your own driving, take it slow and watch out for the tour buses. These sights are listed in clockwise order, though you can do the route in the opposite direction too.

Samoeng Town
เมืองสะเมิง

Once you get to Samoeng Town you will have to connect to Route 1096, but if you're hungry or want to rest your gluteus maximi this is a good place to stop. Samoeng is a small village where dense jungle crowds the margins, seemingly waiting for its chance to reclaim the site. It has one main street with a few shops and restaurants where you can stretch your legs.

Afterward head back to the loop road and continue onto Route 1096; this is the Mae Rim–Samoeng Road and it's where you'll find the best attractions in the loop. If you just want to visit Samoeng and aren't too concerned about seeing the surrounding area, you can get one of a few daily non-air-conditioned buses from Chang Phueak Bus Station in Chiang Mai.

Queen Sirikit Botanic Garden
สวนพฤกษศาสตรสมเด็จพระนางเจาสิริกิติ

Nesting high in its mountain niche, the ambrosial Queen Sirikit Botanic Garden (100 Mu 9, Km 12 Mae Rim, tel. 05/329-8171, www.qsbg.org/index_E.asp, 8:30 A.M.–4:30 P.M. daily, 40B adult, 10B child, 100B vehicle) is an attraction that always rates highly with visitors to Chiang Mai. Nature lovers, horticultural hobbyists, children, and those who simply relish fresh air and beautiful surroundings are likely to enjoy poking amidst the exotic and sometimes bizarre plant species, and investigating the botanical projects being carried on by the scientists researching here. The best time to visit is between November

and March when you'll find the most flowers in bloom.

The gardens are located just a few minutes down from Route 1096 heading from Samoeng on your right. As you approach you'll see Doi Suthep Pui National Park on your left. Originally named the Mae Sa Botanical Gardens, the site opened to the public in 1992 and was renamed in 1994 to honor the current queen; it is the first project of its kind in Thailand. Many pursuits aimed at preserving and propagating rare and valuable plant species are carried out at the facility, as well as some insect studies such as a firefly conservation effort.

Elephant Camps
ปางช้างแมสา

There are a handful of so-called elephant camps along the Mae Sa Loop,, but the **Mae Sa Elephant Camp** (ปางช้างแมสา, on Route 1096 about 8 km from Route 107 heading west, tel. 05/320-6247, www.maesaelephant camp.com, 7 A.M.–4 P.M. daily, elephant shows 8 A.M., 9:40 A.M., 1:30 P.M. daily) is considered one of the best and most responsible among them. On March 13, National Thai Elephant Day, the park puts on the world's largest elephant buffet, Lanna *kantoke* style, and all 70 of their elephants are invited. The camp's founder, Choochart Kalmapijit, established the park in 1976 by purchasing elephants that had no commercial value from across the country. He later launched a very successful breeding program to battle the animal's rapidly dwindling numbers, and to help ensure a future for the Asian Elephant in Thailand. If you leave Chiang Mai no later than 9 A.M., and save Samoeng and the botanic garden for afterward, you should be in time to catch the morning elephant show with a bathing session for the stars, who aren't above shooting a playful jet of water at anyone in range. There are usually a couple of brave baby elephants who will come over to see if they can get a few pieces of banana or sugar cane from their lovestruck audience; don't worry—vendors will be on hand to provide the willing with these goodies. After the bathing, the animals assemble in the arena where they perform acts designed to showcase their strength and coordination; you will see them moving large logs as their ancestors would have done hundreds of years ago for the Lanna Kingdom, dancing and playing music, and demonstrating their uncanny painting skills, but the best part is the elephant soccer game where the participants will amaze you with their coordination and usually provide a few laughs to boot.

After the show you can sign up to go for a short jungle trek on the back of one of these giants and enjoy the singular experience of perching Lanna nobility as you sway along with your lumbering mount, taking in the exotic sights and sounds of the jungle while your mahout talks quietly to his charge; it's an adventure that only a severe allergy to elephants should prevent you from trying. The cost is 1,000B for an hour of your elephant's time, and two people can easily share; those who are nervous about the ride or have motion sickness can choose the half-hour ride instead.

Before you leave the camp, swing by their gallery and exhibition hall where you'll see some great photographs of newborn elephants, a collection of traditional elephant hunting weapons, and most wonderfully, art created by the facility's remarkably skilled painting elephants—it will definitely give you something to think about. You might expect that a painting pachyderm would create at best a colorful yet abstract work, "splash of red there and a streak of black over here" sort of stuff, right? Not so! These very clever elephants not only casually produce obvious landscapes, they do a better job of it than a lot of humans could, with true-to-life color schemes and deliberate dimension and depth. In fact Mae Sa's artists earned a Guinness World Record award and Ripley's Believe It or Not distinction in 2005 when they produced the world's largest and most expensive painting ever created by elephants. Entitled "Cool Wind, Swirling Mist, Charming Lanna," the astonishing eight-panel, 12-meter-long modern impressionist work depicting the northern Thai

countryside was painted in six hours by eight elephants working side by side, contributing a panel each. Incredibly the artists seemed to have all been on the same wavelength about what they were painting because the transitions between one elephant's section and the next are virtually seamless. The painting sold for 1.5 million baht and was then donated back to Thailand in two parts, one as a gift to the Thai government, and one to be displayed in Mae Sa Camp's gallery where it can still be seen.

If you are not quite ready to part with elephants yet, or if you just want something bizarre and eye-catching for your resume, Mae Sa also offers one-, two-, and three-day mahout courses aimed at visitors to Chiang Mai. You can get up close and personal with the elephants, learning about their biology and diet, and how to take care of them along with how to give basic commands. You are given a proper mahout's outfit and will spend time splashing around trying to bathe them and learning how to ride; at the end you are presented with a "novice mahout" certificate. The two- and three-day courses include accommodation and a bonus Thai cooking lesson—cooking for people, that is.

If you only manage to visit the Queen Sirikit Botanic Garden and the elephant camp then you will have covered the two most impressive attractions, but there are a lot of other options on the route between Samoeng and Mae Rim. If you want to stay out in the mountains rather than in Chiang Mai, this area is a good choice; you will have no trouble finding something to suit you among the bungalows, guesthouses, hotels, and resorts located both on Mae Rim–Samoeng Road and in Mae Rim Town.

If you have the time, you can find the **Mae Sa Snake Farm** (804 Mae Rim–Samoeng Rd., tel. 05/386-0719, shows at 11:30 A.M., 2:15 P.M., and 3:30 P.M. daily, 200B adult, 100B child), where they keep snakes from across the country and operate breeding and venom-collecting programs. Their collection includes a giant python and several large and dangerous cobras.

Original Monkey Center
ศูนย์ฝึกลิง

Two kilometers west of the snake farm is the Original Monkey Center (296 Mu 1, Mae Rim–Samoeng Rd., tel. 05/329-8818, shows 11 A.M., 12:15 P.M., 1:15 P.M., and 2:15 P.M. daily, 200B adult, 100B child), which was started when the owner got the idea of buying a few monkeys and training them to help him pack tamarind fruits for market, which turned out to be not only very successful but also hilarious to his neighbors. This inspired him to buy and train more monkeys for work and entertainment purposes, and in fact if you have a monkey that has been misbehaving, you can bring it here for a few classes to improve his behavior and maybe teach him a new skill.

Twelve kilometers along from Mae Rim is the **Mae Sa Valley Crafts Village** (6/2 Mu 2, Pongyang, tel. 05/329-0052, maesa1@ ksc.th.com, 9:30 A.M.–9:30 P.M. daily), a fairyland of succulent greenery dripping with impossible quantities of colorful flowers. You can stroll around the grounds, check out their working farm, and visit the artisans who make *sa* paper, fashion umbrellas, paint ceramics, and practice traditional culinary arts in the village. If you want to try your hand at their trades, half-day courses are available from 600 to 1,200B with all materials provided; you can of course take your creations home with you.

Mae Taeng, Chiang Dao
แมแตง, เชียงดาว

If you continue north on Route 107 from Mae Rim (just east of Samoeng) it will lead you deep into the north Thai countryside, past farms and small villages and a few of the more rugged sightseeing venues such as jungle trekking, river rafting, and spelunking in some rather impressive caves. It will eventually leave you at the town of Fang, 151 kilometers from Chiang Mai and very close to the northernmost part of Thailand and its border with Myanmar. From there you can take the smaller Route 1089 a little further to the border town of Ban Tha Ton. If city life isn't your scene and you want to get away from the tourist traps and into something

100 percent Thai, you might consider sojourning up this route. This is also the best direction to head if you want to visit the Hill Tribe Villages of the Lahu, Lisu, Karen, and Hmong people, which can be done in a single day or with overnight stays either nearby or right in the villages with the tribes.

Mae Taeng District is on the rise as a popular trekking area and its thick jungles, towering mountains, and magnificent rivers are beginning to draw their fair share of adventure tourists. A number of organized tours have begun to come out this way and there are lots of interesting options for checking out this relatively pristine part of Chiang Mai Province. Regular mountain biking, hiking, and whitewater-rafting tours leave from Chiang Mai city, as well as daily private and group tours offering an air-conditioned vehicle and driver; one of the most-loved of these is the elephant trek/hill tribe/bamboo river rafting/oxcart ride ménage à quatre offered by many tour agents. If your time budget is small this is a good option for experiencing the best excursions in the quickest way possible. If you can only fit in one hill tribe village on your trip, make sure it's the **Long Neck Karen** (Karen Padaung), both for the amazing image cast by their traditional ensemble and because their way of life is threatened, possibly making a visit with them a once-in-a-lifetime opportunity. You're not likely to be disappointed by any of the other tribes, however, who wear striking cultural dress and keep to their fascinating traditional lifestyles perched on the mountainsides all throughout this area.

This can be an interesting drive and taking a rental vehicle up this way isn't difficult, although some of the roads leading to the tribal villages are in rough condition and require four-wheel drive or a motorcycle to traverse. No matter how you go about it, you'll either start out on Route 107 from the north, as you would going to Mae Rim, or leave town from the south on Route 108 taking the path to Samoeng and then joining Route 107 via the Mae Rim–Samoeng Road. If you go via Samoeng you'll be taking the slightly longer scenic route, but if you haven't done this day trip already and you have the time, it's easy to add the key sights located on Mae Rim–Samoeng Road to your venture north, overnighting in Mae Rim or Mae Taeng before continuing north. Accommodation and basic amenities are available in most of the towns on the road to Fang, but selection dwindles as you get further from the Chiang Mai tourist belt, and it's a good idea to get your cash before leaving the city as some of the smaller towns do not have ATMs and many have only one, leaving you few options if anything goes wrong. Also remember to fill up on gas whenever you leave a town site because there are very few gas stations on the highway.

A short 23 kilometers north of Mae Rim (39 km from Chiang Mai) lies the town of Mae Taeng, whose primary claim to fame is its convenient location close to many of the popular trekking routes; it's also the last major town before Chiang Dao, 32 kilometers further north. This is a good place to stop for a bite to eat and to pick up any necessities before hitting the attractions strung out along the highway just north of the town.

Wat Tung Luang (วัดทุ่งหลวง) presents a rather unusual spectacle that may not be to all tastes, but it has managed to bring the otherwise unremarkable temple some notoriety. This was the home of the much venerated monk Khru Ba Thammachai, who passed away in 1988 at age 73. The buildings of this *wat* have been brightly decorated in his honor and there is a very lifelike wax model of him in the *wiharn*. The unusual and slightly macabre feature however is the view of his body available through the glass top of his coffin, still standing to the right of the wax effigy.

Heading north again you'll come to an east turn off at Km 43 that signals the beginning of a stretch of elephant camps, some of them offering a range of trekking options including the popular elephant, raft, and oxcart adventure. Most expect bookings through a tour agent, but if you've made no prior arrangements you may still be able to manage a drop-in if they have the space. Three good ones are the **Mae Taeng**

Elephant Park (ปางช้างแม่แตง, 35/1 Mun Mueang Rd., Mae Taeng, tel. 05/320-6459, 8 A.M.–2 P.M. daily, www.elephanteco.com), **Mae Taman Rafting** (ล่องแพแม่ตะมาน, tel. 05/329-7060, show at 9:30 A.M.), and the **Elephant Nature Park & Safari** (booking through Gem Travel, tel. 05/327-2855 and 05/381-8744, show at 10 A.M.), which all charge around 500B for the elephant show and a short trek by elephant, oxcart, and raft.

For a rewarding experience outside the usual elephant-camp fare you can sign up for a visit to the award-winning **Elephant Nature Park** (tel. 05/381-8754, www.elephantna turepark.org), a conservation facility where instead of riding the animals and watching them display their training you get a crash course in elephant care and conservation. This park has gained worldwide acclaim for its conservation efforts and has been featured in documentaries and showcased on the Discovery Channel, and the park's owner, Lek, even appeared in *Time* magazine. It's a full day starting with a pickup from your hotel, then you'll have a chance to personally hand-feed the elephants and then head into the river to give them their bath (2,500B including lunch). They also offer more immersive two- and three-day programs that involve staying right at the park in their clean but basic huts, and of course even more time with the herd; all visits must be booked in advance via their website.

Chiang Dao is a small market town that serves the local Lisu, Hmong, Akha, and Padaung hill tribe villagers, and it's the halfway point to Fang; this is about as far as you would want to come if you are planning to return to Chiang Mai the same day. The Chiang Dao market is a nice example of a bright, noisy, pungent 100 percent Thai agrarian market and you won't find much in the way of tourist goods here. A visit can be a real eye opener, but try to get in early because these early-to-rise-early-to-bed farmers tend to roll up the sidewalk early. If you go east from Chiang Dao, past Wat Indra, you can check out some traditional lowland villages, and if you have four-wheel drive you can continue up to the plateau beyond where there are a number of hill tribe villages. The leafy dips and peaks of Doi Chiang Dao are considered to be one of the most beautiful vistas in Chiang Mai Province and you'll get a number of viewpoints on your way into town, it's worth taking a moment here and there to stop and breathe it all in.

What really draw travelers however are the **Chiang Dao Caves** (Tham Chiang Dao), a vast maze of natural tunnels extending as far as 16 kilometers into Doi Chiang Dao. To get to the caves, follow the main road through town until you see a sign for the caves. Bear left and continue on for another seven kilometers. Many consider this to be the best of the sights on this stretch of highway. The site is viewed as sacred to local Buddhists and is an active site of worship; along with a trove of spectacular natural formations many Buddha images repose in silent meditation. The legend of the Chiang Dao caves centers around a hermit-sage who lived on Doi Chiang Dao for a thousand years, eventually becoming so intimate with the deity realm that he was able to convince some mythical beings to endow the caverns with seven magical wonders: a solid-gold Buddha with a stream flowing from its pedestal, a cache of divine textiles, a mystical lake, a *naga* citadel, an immortal elephant, and the tomb of the hermit himself. According to the locals these arcane treasures are hidden so deep within the cave system that other than the hermit no one has ever seen them. Of course it wouldn't do you or Dr. Jones any good even if you did find them because as you might expect they're protected by a powerful curse: Apparently anyone attempting to remove so much as a pebble from the caverns is doomed to become hopelessly lost in the warren of tunnels and wander for eternity.

This is not the place to wander away from the well-lit pathways without a guide—there are many kilometers of inky-black tunnels twisted into a confusing labyrinth that even a very good flashlight can't help you to navigate, not to mention the occasional unmarked sudden drop-off. But not to worry, the five caves that are open to the public are safe and well maintained, some with electric lighting, and guides are waiting with oil lamps to take you through for 100B per group. At the main entrance, just five kilometers west of town, you will find the stairs ascending to the caves and a pool of spring water sporting some rather large over-fed fish; you can purchase some fish food and add to their obviously ample diet if you like before paying your 10B admission fee and carrying on to the caves. Exploring two of the caves, **Tham Phra Non** and **Tham Seua Dao,** on your own is easy with electric lighting to accompany you, but **Tham Ma, Tham Kaeo,** and **Tham Nam** are dark, so pick up one of the waiting guides who can tell you a little bit about the different formations you'll see as you clamber around sweeping caverns, squeeze through a few tight spaces, and even crawl from time to time. Obviously anyone suffering from claustrophobia should probably sit this one out, but if you can stomach the occasionally uncomfortable conditions you'll be rewarded with some very weird and wonderful geology naturally sculpted into over a hundred strange and beautiful formations.

There are some basic guesthouses in Chiang Dao; just outside of town is the **Marisa Resort and Spa** (304 Mu 4, Muang-Ngai, Chiang Dao, tel. 05/337-5517, 1,600B), a collection of wooden bungalows and rooms in a lush, green setting overlooking a small river with nice mountain views from most of the rooms. Rooms and bathrooms are all comfortable, clean, and modern, though not quite up to boutique-hotel standards. The stand-alone villas, which can accommodate small families or groups traveling together, are a bargain and may persuade you to use the resort as a base for exploring the rest of the region.

After Chiang Dao you'll have a green expanse of rice fields, jungle, and towering mountains for company as you press on to Fang, but at this point you're out of the tourist zone and the last 80 kilometers don't offer much to stop for. There is however an opportunity to check out a natural Thai teakwood forest 10 kilometers north of Chiang Dao at the junction with Route 1150. Head east down 1150 for a pleasant few minutes to see these trees that have played a key role in Thai art and culture from the times of Lanna to today.

DOI ANG KHANG
ดอยอ่างขาง

Part of the **Mae Fang National Park,** Doi Ang Khang is one of Thailand's most beautiful mountains, and at 585 meters above sea level it has an unusually temperate climate year-round, which local farmers have traditionally made use of for growing crops that are unsuited to the warmer environment found everywhere else. The apricots, peaches, and plums grown on its slopes are considered rather exotic among Thais, and carrots, herbs, and salad greens thrive here along with flower farms turning out carnations, roses, asters, and chrysanthemums. The unique conditions have resulted in Doi Ang Khang being used as something of an agricultural petri dish, with all kinds of crops being brought to the mountain to see if they will grow. There is a **Royal Agricultural Project** station (Ban Khum, Mae Ngon, tel. 05/345-0107, 30B/person and 50B/vehicle admission) at the summit where research into various substitution crops to replace opium for the hill farmers is ongoing. The station has public gardens and sells produce, literally showcasing the fruits of their labors; there are also restaurants and even a guesthouse (800–900B) to receive visitors. Unfortunately the mountain's ability to produce exotic flora has prompted over-cultivation and deforestation, although regulation has been put in place and the damaged areas are beginning to come back. An interesting side effect of all these ventures and projects has been remarkably diverse forests, with leafy escapees growing in among the original complement of plants on the mountain. This in turn has attracted a huge variety of birds that come to the mountain to feast on the array of fruits—in fact Doi Ang Khang is generally considered to be one of the best spots for bird-watching in northern Thailand, and it's also pretty good for wildflowers.

The mountain is home to a number of **Lahu, Lisu,** and **Hmong** hill tribe villages, and there are even a few **Yunnanese settlements** transplanted from China. If you pack along a decent map you can visit them and even hike a few of the trekking trails without needing a guide. Maps are available in Fang and at the military checkpoint on Route 1249 that takes you into Mae Fang National Park.

Most people make for the summit by turning east off of Route 107 at Km 137 (16 km before Fang Town) and driving the steep, jungle-hemmed 24 kilometers to the top. Adventurists, however, might be interested in braving the more scenic and more rugged back road. Route 1178 departs Route 107 just north of Chiang Dao and winds its way north past archaic mountain villages and agrarian vistas, meandering along a ridge for 48 kilometers to the top of Doi Ang Khang. This is not a good place to get stuck or have a breakdown, so if you go this way use common sense, pack along the things you might need, and be extra careful following wet weather. Despite (or possibly because of) its rustic quality, it's an exciting route to take to get to Fang. Make sure to connect to Route 1340 (keep heading north) at its junction with 1178; then depart the mountaintop via Route 1249 to return to Route 107 and the last short northward hop to Fang Town.

Fang
ฝาง

All the way at the north terminus of Route 107, for most people Fang village is only a brief stop on their way to bigger destinations, but it has a few interesting elements of its own if you have a bit of time on your hands. You will find most of the basic amenities including a few banks, some currency-exchange services, restaurants and accommodation, and you can wander about exploring the back streets, where odd local shops wait with their dusty wares crammed into the recesses of the wooden buildings. Nearby expanses of Mae Fang National Park shelter a few Karen and Mien hill tribe villages, and the Fang Hot Springs that simmer sulfurously just eight kilometers northwest of town. Apart from the apparatus of the geothermal energy station, an Israeli-built sustainable power project, the four-hectare forested hot springs area is an attractive and pristine location for an outing; many locals come here on weekends to picnic and enjoy some quality time with their families. The park is literally bursting with springs and there are over 50 spots where hot water escapes to the surface in temperatures ranging from 40 to 100 degrees Celsius. Many of the fonts shoot from the earth either continuously or at intervals, sending steaming jets of water meters into the air and shedding the pungent aroma of sulfur. Numerous daily minibuses depart Chiang Mai's Chang Phueak Bus Station for the three-hour drive to Fang.

Tha Ton
ทาตอน

Only 32 kilometers north of Fang on Route 1089, tiny Tha Ton is actually surprisingly well set up to handle tourists, and given the choice most people prefer to stay in this charming, colorful little town rather than in Fang. Nestled in its valley and clinging to the banks of the Mae Kok River, this jungle-soaked hamlet manages to attract travelers mainly because of its daily 3–6 hour (depending on river conditions) longtail boat rides to Chiang Rai (12:30 P.M., 200B) that take you past hill tribe villages, green soaring mountains, and steamy lowland jungle so tranquil and beautiful that it almost makes your heart ache a little. With the number of people passing through on their way to and from Chiang Mai and Chiang Rai, it was only a matter of time before guesthouses, restaurants, and even full-fledged resorts sprang up to serve them. You often see hill tribe people about town and the surrounding area is full of their villages. This is a great place to plan a do-it-yourself visit, most people rent a bicycle or motorcycle but you can even simply hoof it right from town and hike to some the closest ones.

There are a number of tour agents operating in town, and all kinds of organized and informal trekking, biking, and rafting adventures set out daily to take in the surrounding countryside. There are a handful of small tour outfitters (available by phone only) in the town of Tha Ton, including **Thaton Tours** (tel. 05/337-3143), **Tip Travel** (tel. 05/345-9312), **Baan Thaton** (tel. 05/345-9138), and **Ban Tha Ton Boat Club** (tel. 05/345-9427). All can arrange half- to multiday tours with hill tribe visits, hiking, and river rafting. Expect to pay around 1,000B per day, which will include basic accommodations in the jungle and food and drink.

Wat Tha Ton is the local monastery and is reached by a staircase that takes you up to its perch on the mountainside, with impressive ornamental gardens and wonderful views of the valley. The monks give English-language meditation classes each evening and work to treat people with drug addictions, most often hill farmers trying to get free of opium. The giant bell at the monastery is loud enough to be heard all through the valley, and is rung once at 4 A.M. to wake up the monks, and once at 6 A.M. to signal the period of alms collecting.

One very popular, if fairly rugged, excursion is the river route to Chiang Rai spread out over three days, during which you cruise aboard a bamboo "house" raft, consisting of a lashed bamboo platform with a small bamboo hut erected on one end of it. During your journey you sleep and dine on board or at hill tribe villages; your raft comes with a captain and cook, so all you have to do is take it easy and take it in. The trip will cost you a few thousand baht per person and there are usually at least four passengers to a boat. Though not for the faint of heart or sensitive of rump, the excursion scores pretty big points for excitement while failing in basic comforts, and promises a pretty unforgettable experience for those who dare. You can book a raft through one of the tour agents, or simply go down to the dock and see if you can work out a deal with one of the boats' owners.

If you're planning on making the trip from Chiang Mai a multiday affair, the **Thaton River View Resort** (302 Baan Thaton, Mae Ai, tel. 05/337-3173–5, www.thaton-riverview-resort.chiangmai-chiangrai.com, 1,400B) is a lovely place to spend the night. The resort is set on the river and the mountain backdrop is breathtaking. Rooms are comfortable and clean, though not luxurious, but the views make up for it. There is a great restaurant on the premises, too.

There are a few non-air-conditioned buses running daily from Chiang Mai's Chang Phueak Bus Station. The trip takes four hours and this is not the most pleasant option, but it will work for some travelers.

Chiang Rai Province จังหวัดเชียงราย

While the town of Chiang Rai doesn't have enough attractions within it to hold your attention for too long, the surrounding area is beautiful and far less traveled than Chiang Mai Province, making it a good choice if you want to enjoy the scenery and meet people from the surrounding hill tribes.

Chiang Rai is the country's northernmost province (barely beating out Chiang Mai by about 32 kilometers), a generally mountainous area bordered on the north by Burma on one side and Laos on another. This border region was once notoriously known for its drug trade but now is better known for its cooler, mountain weather, hill tribes, and beautifully crafted goods, as well as good regional agricultural products such as coffee and tea. It is a region not to be missed, especially for those who like the outdoors and are curious about the different ethnic groups living in the region.

Even if you only have a few days the scenery and sights around Chiang Rai are an important addition to your trip. The most beautiful thing about Chiang Rai is the surrounding area, and the city is small and it's easy to hit the main roads. Do not hesitate to rent a motorbike or even a bicycle; many of the surrounding sights are only 16 kilometers from town and the roads are in good condition and far from busy.

CHIANG RAI TOWN
เมืองเชียงราย

Less developed than its sister to the south, Chiang Rai is smaller and more intimate than Chiang Mai, and if you were disappointed to find so much traffic and commotion in Chiang Mai, you may find Chiang Rai more to your liking. Most of the town can be covered on foot

and there are many refreshing little sidewalk cafés to fortify you as you stroll its pleasant streets and explore its curious *sois*. Though the atmosphere is distinctly Thai, fellow travelers, tour agencies, guesthouses, and a handful of international restaurants are still easily found. Here you can enjoy the benefits of being a bit further off the well-beaten tourist track without sacrificing key comforts and conveniences. Many travelers base themselves in the town and set off on single or multiday treks through the mountains from here.

Sights
If you're spending a day or two in Chiang Rai, make sure to check out a few of the town's *wats* and museums. The most important historically is **Wat Phra Kaeo** (Trairat Rd. near Ratdetdamrong Rd., daylight hours), where the emerald Buddha that now resides in Bangkok's Wat Phra Kaeo was found in the 15th century. The little green Buddha, which has been replaced by a replica, is one of the most important Buddha images in Thailand and perhaps the most important for the ruling Chakri Dynasty, and is said to have been made more than 2,000 years ago in Sri Lanka and then moved from there to present-day Burma and Cambodia, then Ayutthaya and finally Chiang Rai before it was hidden away under plaster, only to be discovered by a monk after a fortuitous strike of lightning. There's speculation that the provenance of the figure is not what common myth would have everyone believe, but no one doubts that its presence in this *wat* was historically documented as far back as 700 years ago. The figure didn't stay long here; its journey continued on to Wat Chedi Luang in

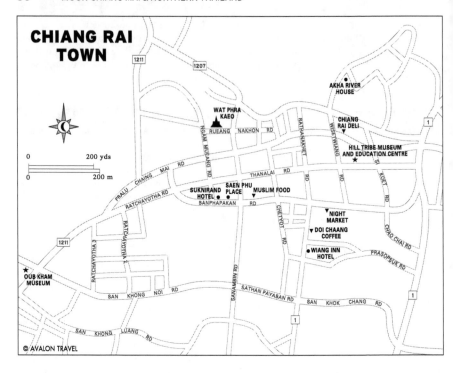

Chiang Mai and then on to Laos, not finding its current home in Bangkok until the 18th century. Still, Wat Phra Kaew is considered an important temple. The complex itself has been renovated over the centuries but remains a largely wooden structure, decorated with red and ornate gold details. Surrounding the *wat* is a nice garden with bamboo copses.

The **Hill Tribe Museum and Education Centre** (620/35 Thanalai Rd., 3rd fl., tel. 05/371-9167, www.pda.or.th/chiangrai/hilltribe_museum.htm, 9 A.M.–6 P.M. Mon.–Fri., 10 A.M.–6 P.M. Sat.–Sun., 50B) is a must-stop if you are going to be doing any trekking to hill tribes in the region. Run by the Population and Community Development Association, the small museum offers a wealth of information about the cultures of the different ethnic groups living in the region as well as some interesting exhibits on the cultivation of opium. The PDA also runs nonprofit tours of surrounding villages, all of which are designed to reduce the negative impact of tourism on these small communities while bringing as much of the monetary profit from them directly to the villagers. If scheduling permits, this is probably the most responsible way to see the hill tribes. If not, supporting the PDA's community development projects is a piece of cake—the shop at the center has a great selection of goods at more than reasonable prices. There is a particularly good variety of different woven goods—bags, pouches, wallets, even bottle-holders, representing different hill tribe styles. They also have a wide selection of gifts, including nutcrackers and garlic presses made from forest wood.

If you're interested in Lanna Kingdom art, stop into the private **Oub Kham Museum** (พิพิธภัณฑ์อูบคำ, 81/1 Thanon Na Khai, Rop Wiang district, tel. 05/371-3349, 10 A.M.–9 P.M. daily, 200B) just outside of town. Set

village in the mountains of northern Thailand

in a beautiful garden, the museum houses a private collection of art from the Lanna Kingdom, including jewelry, devotional art, and housewares.

A little bit outside of town but worth the few-kilometer drive west of Chiang Rai is **Mae Fa Luang Art and Cultural Park** (313 Mu 7, Ban Pa Ngiew, tel. 05/371-1968, 10 A.M.–6 P.M. Tues.–Sun., 200B). The art center, a project of the king's late mother to preserve Lanna culture, contains displays of devotional and secular art and artifacts from the Lanna Kingdom. Objects include 19th-century murals, Buddha images, and household objects, and there are also some very large carved wood pieces within the park. The collection is housed on the grounds of a 26-hectare botanical garden speckled with lily ponds and *sala*. This is a lovely place to spend an afternoon strolling the grounds and enjoying the collection of art.

Food

The **Night Market** (Phahonyothin Rd. and Prasopsuk Rd. next to the bus station, 6–10 P.M. daily) is a great bet for a large selection of inexpensive food, and you'll find dishes from all over the country for sale here. As an added bonus, there always seems to be something going on at the market, be it a local dance performance or even an outdoor movie.

If you want to sit down and eat, try the **Center Point Night Bazaar** (tel. 05/374-0122, 6–11 P.M. daily, 100B) right in the middle of the night market. It may seem a little touristy, but the Thai dishes are exceptionally well prepared. Their Thai menu is massive and includes all sorts of specialties, such as northern food and Isan. Local vegetables are featured often, as is fish. There is an especially good selection of Thai spicy salads, including some less common ones such as pineapple salad and fish *maw*, or Kraphopla (กระเพาะปลา), salad. There are also some Western options if you have the urge for some spaghetti or a tuna sandwich.

This restaurant may have another name in Thai, but the only name on the English sign is **Muslim Food** (407/1 Israparb Rd., tel. 05/371-5296, 7 A.M.–8 P.M. daily, 50B). Regardless of the name, this restaurant serves freshly prepared halal meals.

Who would have thought you could get salami, gouda, blue cheese, and a host of other meats and European cheeses in the northernmost province of Thailand? The authentic **Chiang Rai Deli** (489/3 Utarakit Rd., tel. 08/7175-3477, 1–9 P.M. daily) will remind you of cravings you forgot you had. You can buy their pre-packed blocks of cheese and sausage meat. They even have sauerkraut and pickles(!), and all the important condiments too.

If you're looking for a quick meal, there are two identical nameless typical Thai eateries (421/10 Isaraparb Rd., tel. 05/371-4633, daily) displaying a wide variety of Thai foods—just point and take your pick. They have more interesting dishes such as steamed whole fish and *amok,* a classic Cambodian dish made with either meat or fish and cooked in herbs and a little coconut milk, served in a small banana-leaf bowl. They also have mango with sticky rice and some other sweets. Both places are clean and well lit, making them pleasant for dining, and the Thai staff is friendly.

The atmosphere is lovely at the two **Doi Chaang Coffee** (Rattanakhet Rd., tel. 05/375-2918, and Banphaprakarn Rd., tel. 05/375-2847, 8 A.M.–7 P.M. daily) shops in town. Besides fresh coffee made from locally grown beans, they serve all-day breakfasts at a surprisingly good deal and have a few sandwiches and soups on the menu as well as smoothies and a delicious array of baked goods. If you're looking for a place to hang out and catch up on email, they offer free Wi-Fi, too.

Accommodations

This guesthouse, owned by the same Akha people who run tours to neighboring hill tribes, is a great, inexpensive option in Chiang Rai: **Akha River House** (423/25 Mu 21 Soi 1, Kholoy Rd., tel. 08/9997-5505, www.akha hill.com, 150B) offers comfortable, well-designed rooms and bungalows set right on the river in a very scenic, verdant area of Chiang Rai. Rooms are not luxurious but surprisingly nice considering how inexpensive they are. Nearly everyone who stays here books one of the tours, which may account for the low price.

Saen Phu Place (389 Banphaprakarn Rd., tel. 05/371-7300–9, 650B) is a large, pleasant modern hotel with all modern amenities. Price includes a buffet breakfast with basic American items as well as some Thai food (don't expect an omelet station). There is a disco bar in the basement if you feel like letting loose later in the evening, though noise doesn't seem to be a problem if you want to sleep instead. There is plenty of parking and it's conveniently located f you have your own transport; it's just a few minutes to the Night Bazaar or center of town, yet with easy access to the main road.

Suknirand Hotel (424/1 Banphaprakarn Rd., tel. 05/371-1055, 450B) is a bit more small and charming than Saen Phu Place as the rooms are only on two levels and the property is set back from the road. Rooms are comfortable and clean and up to Western standards, though not particularly luxurious. There are also fan-only rooms here that are about 30 percent less expensive than those with air-conditioning. This hotel is very well located for seeing the town's sights.

Walk into the lobby of the **Wiang Inn Hotel** (893 Phaholyothin Rd., tel. 05/371-1533, 2,000B) and you'll forget you are in Chiang Rai, or even Thailand for that matter. This is probably the most Western place in town; they even have a hotel bar right in the lobby. This is a good choice if you want large, clean rooms and the ease of staying at a big hotel and don't mind going without the charm of smaller properties.

The Legend (124/15 Mu 21, Kohloy Rd., tel. 05/391-0400, www.thelegend-chian grai.com, 3,900B) is a beautiful boutique hotel just one and a half kilometers out of the center of town. All the rooms are done in a Thai-tropical style. Bathrooms have showers separate from toilets, all done in plenty of natural stone and natural light. The villas are particularly lovely with their own whirlpool tubs. The hotel has everything you would expect—spa, two restaurants, and impeccable service—and it also offers a free shuttle to the Night Bazaar, as well as rents bikes and tricycle taxis.

© SUZANNE NAM

hill tribe children and hikers in a village rest stop

Getting There

With daily direct flights from Bangkok on Thai Airways, Bangkok Airways, Air Asia, and One-Two-Go, it's easy to visit Chiang Rai. The **Chiang Rai Airport** is just a few kilometers out of town; if your hotel or guesthouse isn't picking you up, there are taxis waiting.

If you are coming from Chiang Mai, you can board a three-hour bus from the city; there are more than a dozen official government buses and private buses departing throughout the day and an air-conditioned bus will cost under 200B.

Driving is a great option for those who want to tour the area and enjoy the scenery. The drive from Chiang Mai takes under three hours but there's a lot to do along the way, so if you are planning to use a car make sure to allow time to stop. The way to travel is to take the **Mae Sa Loop** from Chiang Mai. You'll only get to do half of it, and whether you choose the top or bottom, you'll have to turn off onto Route 118 heading east, then Highway 1 heading north, to get to Chiang Rai.

Getting Around

The city itself is easily walkable, and there's no need for motorized transport if you're just going from your guesthouse to a restaurant or one of the city's sights. If you're staying out of the city or want to visit something farther off, you'll need to hire a *tuk tuk* or taxi.

Outside of the city you'll need to either hire a taxi or get your own transport to enjoy all of the sights and scenery. There are numerous shops renting motorbikes, otherwise there is an **Avis** (tel. 05/379-3827, www.avisthailand.com) and a **National Car Rental** (tel. 05/379-3683) in the airport.

DAY TRIPS FROM CHIANG RAI TOWN

There are many day trips to be taken from Chiang Rai, and dozens of tour companies and guesthouses in the city to take you there. The most common itinerary for a multiday trek starting in Chiang Rai involves trekking out to one of the nearby Lahu, Akha, Karen, or Hmong villages, spending a couple of hours visiting an elephant camp and riding elephants, and some rafting on a nearby river (longer treks may even take you as far as the Mekong River on the border with Laos). As these are group tours, it is not possible to customize them, however if you are interested in just doing some rafting or hiking, you can arrange a one-day tour to do so. PDA's nonprofit tours are a great choice for their promise of responsible tourism, and **Akha Hill House** (423/25 Mu 21, Soi 1, Kholoy Rd., tel. 08/9997-5505, www.akha-hill.com) is another great choice. The group of Akha have a small guesthouse in town and run single- and multiday treks to a base in their Akha hill tribe community about 24 kilometers from the city.

CHIANG SAEN AND THE GOLDEN TRIANGLE
เชียงแสนและสามเหลี่ยมทองคำ

After reading about the wilder past of the Golden Triangle, you may be surprised to find Chiang Saen, a basically normal-looking town with a nice little museum and some interesting ruins. Set on the banks of the Mekong River, the area has probably been populated nearly continuously for thousands of years according to archaeological evidence. During the 14th century, it was a small walled town with more than 70 temples within its boundaries; if you walk around you're more likely to see scattered ruins from that era than poppies.

Sights

Most people pass through Chiang Saen on their way north to the heart of the Golden Triangle, but if you're in the city stop into the **Chiang Saen National Museum** (702 Phahonyothin Rd., tel. 05/377-7102, 9 A.M.–4 P.M. Wed.–Sun., 30B), housed next to **Wat Chedi Luang.** The museum houses mostly Lanna art from the 14th through 16th centuries, including some excellent examples of the era's style of Buddha statuary.

About eight kilometers outside of the city is the **Hall of Opium** in **Golden Triangle Park** (Mu 1, Ban Sop Ruak, Wiang, tel. 05/378-4444, www.doitung.org, 8:30 A.M.–4 P.M. Tues.–Sun.), a large museum chronicling the

history of opium in the region. The exhibits are well done and yield some fascinating information about the economic role of poppy cultivation in the region, the political role opium has played in East-West relations, as well as the drug trade in general. The museum and 16-hectare park surrounding it are part of the kingdom's efforts to reclaim the region from illegal drug trafficking and give indigenous peoples other opportunities to earn money.

Be careful not to confuse the Hall of Opium with the more modest **House of Opium** (221 Mu 1, Tambon Wiang, tel. 05/378-4060, 7 A.M.–7 P.M. daily, 50B), which conveys roughly the same information, but with much less swish. They use conventional displays, mostly in Thai, and have an interesting selection of opium artifacts, many collected from southern China, and a unique gift shop. The House of Opium focuses specifically on the drug's effect on the local region and peoples, rather than on Asia as a whole, lending an intimate atmosphere to the small museum.

Accommodations

The lodging choices within the city are bleak, but outside of town the options improve considerably. The **Viang Yonok** (201 Mu 3, Yonok, Chiang Saen Lake, tel. 05/365-0444, www.viangyonok.com, 2,200B) is a tiny family-run resort with rustic, comfortable little bungalows and nice grounds including a swimming pool. Although it's not quite a four-star resort, it's a charming and place to stay for a couple of days as you explore the area.

The ◖ **Anantara Golden Triangle** (229 Mu 1, Chiang Saen, tel. 05/278-4084, www.goldentriangle.anantara.com, 8,000B) is one of the nicest resorts in the area (second only to the Four Seasons), with beautiful, spacious rooms decorated with rich Thai fabrics and artwork, all set in a green bamboo forest. There is a full-service spa as well as multiple pools, cooking classes, and a fitness center, but the real attraction is the on-site **elephant camp.** The camp's director scouts out at-risk elephants and their mahouts (particularly those who've been panhandling on the streets of Bangkok)

THE GOLDEN TRIANGLE AND OPIUM TRADE

The rosy-hued blossoms of *Papaver somniferum*, or opium poppy, have been swaying in the mountain breezes of the Golden Triangle region for over a thousand years. Originally mixed into tonics, it was a common ingredient in traditional medicine among locals and was grown and consumed in a remarkably responsible fashion for centuries before trade interests and methods for increasing its potency created the movie-like drama of smugglers, addicts in dark urban rooms, crime lords, and the exotic subculture glamor that some associate with the flower's cultivation today.

Known for much longer in Europe and the Middle East, opium was brought to East Asia by Arab traders around the 7th century. The controversy and excitement really began in the 1700s when the Dutch introduced the practice of smoking opium in tobacco pipes, vastly increasing its potency and hallucinogenic and addictive properties. Abuse of the drug quickly spread through China and the Golden Triangle region, and in 1729 the Chinese emperor placed a ban on its recreational use. About this time European trading companies, most notably the famous British East India Company, recognized the new demand among the addicted Chinese for illegal opium. This solved the growing problem created by low demand for European products in the East, which had forced them to trade silver for expensive commodities such as tea, silk, and porcelain. With vast holdings in India, they began to smuggle Indian opium into China in enormous quantities. The level of addiction mushroomed in China and spread through Southeast Asia, and the demand for it became almost bottomless, with the British East India Company alone unloading an incredible 75 tons of the resin in 1773. The Chinese government's attempts to seize illegal cargo sparked the Opium Wars with England and ended with the ceding of Hong Kong and eventually the legalizing of opium sales. Import of the drug skyrocketed to 4,810 tons by 1858. With so many addicts and hugely inflated prices created by British attempts to monopolize the industry, secret poppy fields became a cash crop for the farmers of the Golden Triangle, with smugglers and drug barons popping up to aid in the distribution of the product.

Medical advances in the 1800s saw opium refined into morphine and then heroin and popularized the practice of administering it by hypodermic injection. It was mixed into all kinds of medicines, such as laudanum, which were distributed legally worldwide with devastating effect. Drug lords soon began to manufacture heroin in hill stations along the Thai-Burmese border, and it made its way in boats and caravans to the northern villages and eventually to Bangkok. In 1914 the India-China opium trade was finally abandoned, increasing the profits of the farmers and hill tribes growing it in the Golden Triangle. Rising addiction and social fallout threw opium and heroin into disfavor in most markets worldwide beginning in the 1920s, and in Thailand it was declared illegal in 1959. Unfortunately this created a black market that sparked the rise of crime syndicates in Bangkok dedicated to smuggling heroin internationally for illegal distribution. With an export market the farmers of the Golden Triangle became the world's largest producers of opium, contributing 70 percent of the world's supply in the 1970s. Efforts by the Thai government, under the patronage of the monarchy, have since driven poppy farms almost to extinction. Programs to help farmers switch to other profitable crops, campaigns to rehabilitate addicts, and the destruction of illicit fields with charges being brought against their growers have nipped the problem in the proverbial bud. Still, there are a few fields that have not yet been wiped out, finding mostly Myanmar customers and netting over 12,000B – nearly US$400 – per pound for those who are willing to risk it. As for the black market mafiosos, it appears that many of them have unfortunately switched to moving amphetamines, but heroin at least is no longer lining their pockets, concluding an exciting and tragic era that has now dispersed like smoke on the wind.

and brings them to the Anantara's camp and mahout village. If you're interested in learning how to work with an elephant, they offer a three-day mahout training program, but otherwise you can just visit the village and watch the elephants. Though this is a great place for a romantic getaway, most children will really enjoy the elephants.

If you really want to splash out, the **Four Seasons Tented Camp** (Chiang Saen, tel. 05/391-0200, www.fourseasons.com/gold entriangle, 45,000B inclusive) is an extreme luxury experience and perhaps the most expensive place to stay in all of Thailand. The camp, set in the middle of the jungle, houses just 15 tents set on a river. Of course, these are not just any tents; they're the size of small homes and surrounded by their own private decks. Accommodations include all meals and drinks as well as excursions and spa treatments.

Getting There

There are **buses** every 15 minutes during the day going from Chiang Rai to Chiang Saen. The journey will take about 90 minutes and costs under 50B. If you are **driving** follow Highway 1 from Chiang Rai to Mae Chan, then turn east onto Route 1016.

MAE SAI AND MAE FA LUANG
แมสายและแมฟาหลวง

As the northernmost town in the kingdom, Mae Sai attracts a fair number of travelers, many curious about the border with Myanmar. But although this tiny town is colorful and bustling, there isn't a whole lot to recommend it. Swirling markets spontaneously materialize in the street on the approach to the crossing, and it can sometimes be difficult to turn around in this area, especially with hundreds of pedestrians and vehicles trying to move between countries. Somewhat more formal shops are folded into the buildings lining this street and there is a hodgepodge of Thai, Lao, and Burmese goods for sale.

You can cross the border yourself if you wish—you will be stamped out of Thailand (negating the balance of any single-entry visas or 30-day visa exemptions) and stamped into Myanmar (500B at the time of writing) for one day only, although you are limited to the border areas. You'll find a very similar constellation of shops and vendors on the other side, but more interesting is watching the legions of local people coming and going between countries, and trying to guess at what they might be up to. On the return to Thailand you'll be stamped back into the country with a new 30-day visa exemption, provided you haven't already exceeded the maximum visa-exempt stay. Regular buses run up this way from Chiang Saen, Chiang Rai, and Chiang Mai, costing 20–150B depending on class.

Mae Fa Luang district is in a sense a memorial to Her Royal Highness, the late Princess Mother Srinakarindra, mother of Thailand's current king. She took a special interest in the welfare of the people living in this region, from the Hill Tribes and their struggle with opium to the border police and their families, and in fact "Mae Fa Luang" was the affectionate nickname given to her by the locals: It means "mother sky royal" in reference to her habit of arriving in the area by helicopter. The Mae Fa Luang Foundation was begun under her patronage and direction, and has been involved in reforestation projects, substitution farming initiatives, cottage-industry preservation and promotion, and education and health-care programs, having a huge impact on the people in this region. Footprints of these efforts are easily found as you travel to the summit of Doi Tung; much of the forest that you see was planted through the efforts of this foundation, and a zoo and arboretum are included among the local projects.

◖ Doi Mae Salong
ดอยแมสะลอง

A favorite place to visit for people traveling to Mae Fa Luang is the hamlet of Doi Mae Salong, unique in both culture and history. The villagers here are not ethnic Thais; they are Yunnan Chinese and their way of life has drifted very little from their native traditions. They have a strange and vibrant past dipped in politics, war, and opium, recent enough to be recalled first-hand by the town's elders. This small town is integrated into the hills, on top of the world at 548 meters, and enchanting landscapes combine with a simplistic agricultural existence to define their mountain sanctuary.

In the 1940s the Kuomintang were a political group opposed to the communist takeover of China, fighting bitterly against them from Yunnan Province in the south. They were eventually forced to flee, escaping to Taiwan and into hidden locations deep within the Myanmar jungle, where they established camps and regrouped to continue their resistance effort. After 12 years of brutal struggle, engaged in opium-funded guerrilla warfare against both the Burmese and Chinese armies, the weary community eventually retreated to neighboring Thailand to regroup in the 1960s. Jungle-savvy, they trekked deep into remote and inaccessible tracts of Chiang Rai's forests, eventually settling in their current location of Mae Salong, precariously close to the territories controlled by the opium warlords of the Golden Triangle. Before long the Yunnanese settlers began their own tidy trade in illegal opium, further isolating them from mainstream Thai society and sparking violent clashes with the private armies of the local crime barons.

Eventually the government initiated its crackdown on the region's drug trade and paved roads rolled up to the village's doorstep, effectively ending the seclusion that had virtually stopped time in this community for decades. The people finally settled into a quiet agrarian existence, enjoying real peace for the first time in many years, and earning the Thai government's symbolic renaming of their village to Santikhiri (Hill of Peace).

Despite the sudden increase in accessibility, however, the villagers still keep to their ethnic roots, making this little town seem like a lost puzzle piece from a Chinese jigsaw. In fact many of its citizens are more recent immigrants from China, who both help to maintain the cultural authenticity of this community and ultimately somewhat erode its unique qualities. The elevation and temperate climate are ideal for the villagers' orchards, Chinese tea,

and traditional herbs, and their produce is very highly regarded. The villagers have even imported their native cherry trees, and the fluttering pink finery of these trees in bloom during December and January is a particular visual delight. The influence of their homeland is also seen in the local cuisine, language, architecture, and sect of Buddhism, and it's interesting simply to stroll around exploring this town. Try not to miss the marketplace where you can see some unusual items for sale, such as loose tea and even dried insects for sale by the pound. Some guesthouses and basic accommodation are available for those who want to take some time out, and it's a great place to sample an authentic southern Chinese meal.

ACCOMMODATIONS

Although many visit this area on a day trip from Chiang Rai, there are a few resorts in the region. The choices are quirky and tend to exploit the connection to China quite aggressively, but they are generally comfortable and charming too. **Mae Salong Resort** (Doi Mae Salong, tel. 05/376-5014, 700B) is a group of wooden hillside bungalows on pretty, green gardens, interspersed with lots of Chinese-style *sala*. Bungalows are basic but clean and there is a large restaurant on the premises.

GETTING THERE

A big part of the charm of a trip up to Mae Salong is the picturesque drive itself, with its captivating panoramas, and there are even a few opportunities to stop along the way. Akha, Hmong, Lisu, and Mien hill tribe villages, some of which are unfortunately pretty touristy, are located on this route, along with Kuomintang tea plantations and a few small waterfalls; if you go with an organized tour from Chiang Rai they will usually include these in their itinerary. It's possible to do your own driving; if you do it's a good idea to pick up a tourist map in the city so that you can do a bit of exploring, but stick to the main roads and attractions because some of the smaller trails lead off into unsafe territory. From Chiang Rai, drive 20 kilometers north along the superhighway to Mae Chan;

once there you turn onto Route 1089, which will take you through the mountains and forests to Mae Salong. If you plan to detour to see any of the hill tribes you should rent a vehicle with four-wheel drive, but if you stick to Route 1089 it isn't necessary. Alternatively you can pick up the bus to Ban Basang from Chiang Rai and then take a *song thaew* to the mountaintop for under 200B for the return trip.

Doi Tung

The other adventure popular with day-trippers to Mae Fa Luang is wandering up the lush and winding road that ascends to the heights of Doi Tung, whose forested limestone peaks stretch to a height of 1,800 meters in places, and where captivating vistas often steal the show from the handful of local attractions. Route 1149 snakes along from the superhighway to the peak of Doi Tung, and other than the copious hairpin turns it's a fairly easy drive; the west turn off to Route 1149 is 40 kilometers north of Chiang Rai and 20 kilometers south of Mae Sai. Doi Tung is very close to Myanmar and an alternate route from Mae Sai is to take Highway 1334, but this road actually straddles the border in places and is a risky choice. Drug traders, Karen rebels, and Thai and Burmese armies are sometimes active in the area, and the fighting on the Myanmar side of the border has been known to spill over into Thailand. If you do go this way, inquire about recent threats at the army checkpoint en route, then drive through without stopping. Most people, however, visit Doi Tung by organized tour, although a rental car or motorcycle is also an option if you don't mind focusing on the road rather than the scenery.

The Princess Mother lived in Switzerland for a number of years while her children were attending school, and she remembered the Swiss countryside fondly after her return to Thailand. Therefore when she decided to build a home on Doi Tung where she could live while working on her social projects, she chose a fusion of Thai and Swiss styles for its design. After her death in 1995, the **Mae Fa Luang Garden and Royal Villa** (Rte. 1149, 7:30 A.M.–5 P.M. daily, 150B includes both garden and villa) were opened to visitors and have become the key attractions on this tour. The villa has been converted to a museum and preserves everything almost exactly as it was when she lived there, but the royal gardens get most people's attention. Again in keeping with the princess's love of the Alps, this garden overflows with flowers that may strike Thais as incredibly exotic, but Westerners will already be familiar with the snapdragons, delphiniums, and begonias displayed here. Despite this, visitors often count this garden among the most beautiful they've seen anywhere in the world, and the delightfully ornate landscaping is very cleverly planned for aesthetic impact. It's worth taking an hour to stroll around, snapping photos and enjoying the pretty grounds and wonderful vistas of the surrounding mountains, and then relaxing with a tea or coffee on the open-air terrace of the cafeteria.

After the Royal Villa the road continues up to the summit and **Wat Doi Tung,** passing breathtaking views of Burmese mountains and landscapes that until recently were crowded with poppy fields. At the top you will find the twin pagodas of **Wat Phra That Doi Tung,** which are small, but very ancient at 1,000 years old, and reputed to contain a relic in the form of a bone from the Buddha's body. This is a very sacred temple for Thais, as well as for local Shan and Chinese Buddhists, and every year many of the faithful make pilgrimages here to the highest point in the province, ritually ringing the row of large bells along the walkway. There are magnificent views of the countryside from up here and you get a sense that the temple's builders once stood where you are standing and admired it themselves so long ago.

Mae Hong Son Province จังหวัดแม่ฮ่องสอน

Set to the west of Chiang Mai Province and bordered by Burma to the east, Mae Hong Son Province still feels like a bit of a frontier region, and although it's not filled with specific sights to see it's a wonderful place to go hiking out into the mountains for a few days or visit some local hill tribes. Although the province is welcoming more and more visitors every year, compared to Chiang Mai and even Chiang Rai, it will probably feel much less touristed—that is, until you get to Pai.

◖ MAE HONG SON
แม่ฮ่องสอน

The City of Three Mists, as Mae Hong Son is nicknamed, has a large population of Shan people who have migrated from the Shan Province of Myanmar. Tucked away in a misty valley whose mountains shelter it from Myanmar to the west and Chiang Mai Province to the east, the people of this region lived for centuries as loosely organized forest farmers with no central government. Only the cacophony of wild elephants and the occasional passage of the Burmese army on their way to attack northern Siam or Ayutthaya interrupted the sleepy populace and their deeply traditional lives. The city itself was founded in the 1800s when Lord Kaeo, a Lanna military chief, was sent to capture and train wild elephants for use in labor. As he traveled he unified the scattered settlers into villages and collected armies of elephants. Finally stopping at a suitable site he established an elephant training camp and village, naming it Baan Mae Rong Son, or "Village of the Elephant Training Camp." The town flourished, attracting Shan hill farmers from the surrounding forests. Until recently the area claimed dense jungle, no modern infrastructure, and cutthroat opium armies; as a result Mae Hong Son has only been accessible to tourists for two decades, and it shows. The tiny town is only a few kilometers across, and as you wander through its bustling produce markets and Burmese-style temples you might feel as though you have stepped back in time, if not for the shiny new hotels and ATMs that have sprung up like daisies in recent years. Frankly, the town itself actually has very little to see other than a few scattered *wats,* but it's a relaxed and scenic spot and a very popular base, as it's served by flights from Bangkok.

Hiking and Rafting

If you've come to Mae Hong Son and you're not planning on enjoying the surrounding jungles, you're probably in the wrong place. But if that's what you're looking for, you'll find plenty of agencies organizing multiday hiking trips that include visiting hill tribe villages and rafting trips on the Pai River. Expect to pay around 1,000B per day for hiking (which includes accommodations and basic food) and a little more per day for a rafting trip.

Accommodations

Mae Hong Son is one of the few popular tourist spots left in Thailand where you can still find a reasonable place to sleep for less than 200B per night. In fact many of the city's accommodations seem geared towards travelers with tighter budgets, and finding plusher places to rest can be a little bit challenging. Though there is nothing extravagant in the city, there are some nice mid-range options that are great values. Most all of the accommodations here can book trekking tours (either they are re-selling them or offering them) and have small restaurants on the premises.

The **Ampa Guest House** (3 Padungmuayto Rd., tel. 05/362-0506, 150B s) is cheap, clean, and charming. The small guesthouse is in an old wooden building and the basic rooms have private bathrooms with cold-water showers. Ampa Guest House is just a five-minute walk from the center of town.

A few kilometers outside of the city is the luxuriant and comfortable **Rim Nam Klang Doi Resort** (108 Ban Huai Deau, tel. 05/361-2142, 600B). Set on the river, with rooms and

mountains of Mae Hong Son Province

stand-alone wooden bungalows, this is a great spot to pick if you're more interested in getting out into nature than anything the small town of Mae Hong Son has to offer.

Though **Piya Guest House** (1/1 Khunlumphrapat Soi 3, tel. 05/361-1260, 600B) isn't as rustic or charming as some of the more inexpensive choices in Mae Hong Son, it is clean, modern, and well located just next to Jongkam Lake in the middle of town. This is a small guesthouse, so you won't get all of the amenities you would find in a big hotel, but you'll still have air-conditioning and television in your room. There is also a lovely garden on the premises.

About a kilometer and a half outside of the center of town are the ◖ **Sang Tong Huts** (Mu 11 Makasanti Rd., tel. 05/362-0680, www.sangtonghuts.com, 700B), a small group of bamboo bungalows with friendly, interesting folks working there. The rooms are clean, beds comfortable, and the bathrooms well kept up. There are also outdoor balconies to lounge on and even a small swimming pool to cool off in. The cheapest rooms here have shared bathrooms, but the larger bungalows have their own bathrooms and are considerably more plush—a great value for the price. There is a small restaurant on the premises serving Thai dishes and fresh baked bread, plus freshbrewed hill tribe coffee in the morning. If you arrange to have dinner prepared for you in advance, you'll be able to help with preparations and take an impromptu cooking class, too.

If you're looking for rustic and charming but don't want to do without a little luxury, pick ◖ **Fern Resort** (64 Mu Bo, Pha Bong, tel. 05/368-6110, www.fernresort.info, 2,500B). There are no compromises here, just large, nicely furnished bungalows with private terraces and a great view of the surrounding jungle and mountains. The resort, a few kilometers out of town, also has a swimming pool and an open-air restaurant with food good enough that you probably won't feel the need to venture out for any of your meals. The staff is very knowledgeable about hiking in the area and there are even some short two-hour trails right around the resort that you can venture out onto without needing to hire a guide.

There is a shuttle to and from town and the resort will arrange free pickup from the airport or bus station.

Food

The first place to find food is the **Morning Market** (Sihanat Bamrung Rd. next to Wat Klang Muang, 5 A.M.–9 A.M. daily), a colorful and bustling market that is mostly not designed for tourists, but rather for people living in the city and the hill tribe villagers from the nearby mountains. The market has fresh fruit and snacks for sale.

Gai Mook (23 Udon Chao Rd., tel. 05/361-2092, 10 A.M.–2 P.M. and 5 P.M.–midnight daily, 100B) has a good selection of Thai dishes available and the setting is a little more upscale than the typical shophouse fare. There are lots of stir-fried dishes here, and seafood too. In fact the menu is not very northern Thai at all, but the food is good and well prepared.

Salween River Restaurant (Sihanat Bamrung Rd., tel. 05/361-2050, 7 A.M.–1 A.M. daily, 100B) is always full of foreign tourists and expats, but don't be put off. The Thai and Shan foods here, particularly the *khao soi* and Shan curries, are very good. If you're in the mood for something more familiar, there are baked goods such as breads and croissants and even spaghetti. Vegetarians will find a few items on the menu made for them, and there's also a book exchange if you want to trade in your novel for another.

Head to **Sunflower Café** (7 Singhana Thoumrung Rd., tel. 05/362-0549, 7:30 A.M.–9 P.M. daily, 120B) to indulge in fresh baked bread and pizza as well as Thai staple dishes. For dessert, enjoy a cappuccino made with hill tribe coffee and a slice of their cheesecake. The café also has a tour agency that organizes multiday hiking tours in the area.

C Bai Fern Restaurant (Khunlum Phrapat Rd., tel. 05/368-6110, 10:30 A.M.–midnight daily, 200B) is part of the same group that owns the Fern Resort, and the restaurant likewise does not disappoint. The menu includes Thai, Shan, and Western dishes and all is served in an open-air wooden dining room.

Getting There

Mae Hong Son is not the easiest area to get to as you'll generally need to pass through Chiang Mai on your way. The city is served by **daily flights** from Chiang Mai on Nok Air and Thai Airways. During high season between December and February, PB Air (www.pbair.com) offers a daily flight from Bangkok to Mae Hong Son.

There are five daily **buses** from Chiang Mai making the seven-to-nine-hour journey for under 350B. If you're coming from Bangkok, there is one scheduled bus from the Northern Bus Terminal per day, leaving in the early evening for the overnight 17-hour ride.

If you're **driving** from Chiang Mai, take Route 108 through Mae Sariang or Route 1095 through Pai. Although the roads are well maintained and the scenery beautiful, you'll encounter a lot of mountains and switchbacks on the way. The drive takes around three hours in a car, longer if you are on a motorbike.

Getting Around

Within the town of Mae Hong Son, the best way to get around is on foot, and the town is small enough that most anyone will feel comfortable walking from place to place.

PAI
ปาย

Time doesn't stand still in Pai, but it certainly slows down a lot, so reset your mental clock—if it's still on city time you might feel a little alarmed here. On the other hand, if you need some help getting out of "work mode," this might be just the place to do it. This humble and idyllic little town offers a slightly bohemian feel for travelers. In fact those travelers appear to have overtaken the little town itself, and you'll probably see five times the number of Western tourists here as you will people actually from the country, and even fewer from the region. A sprinkling of souvenir art shops, open-air bars, and street vendors attempting to "go international" set the stage. Keep an eye out for these seemingly incongruous Thai incarnations designed to catch the tourist's attention, notable among them is KFG, unofficially "Kentucky Fried Gai," *gai* being the Thai word for chicken. Another odd local favorite is "Mama's Falafel," whose recipes, perfected over the years with helpful advice from Israeli visitors, have been so successful that she's been able to upgrade from a street stall to a permanent indoor location. Pai seems to have a sand-in-the-eyes effect on those who visit, almost as though some sort of magic puts to sleep any desire they have to leave. This is reflected in the smorgasbord of people you will find here. Though there is a bit of a hippie subculture in most of the towns in the north, it reaches its zenith in Pai, drawing the most interesting assortment of people as well as the not-so-occasional scent of marijuana wafting through the mountain air. Most of the tourists have come to enjoy some R&R&R—rest, relaxation, and rejuvenation—and you will find many escapists and sojourners who have fallen under the spell; for some a few weeks' holiday becoming a many year, semi-resident affair.

It's not all idyllic and peaceful in Pai, however. Despite the hippie overtones, in recent years there seems to be an increased tendency of visitors to Pai and locals going "off the rails." Though you may only see this in the form of general drunk and disorderly conduct in the late evening (watch for out-of-control scooter drivers!), there have been more serious incidents in this sleepy little town. In late 2007, one unarmed Canadian tourist was shot to death and another seriously injured by an off-duty police officer right in the center of town. The incident has been the subject of much speculation, with some witnesses claiming that the shooting was provoked by violence and others claiming that the officer was drunk and murdered the tourist. So far this incident has not been resolved. Although Pai is generally safe, this is something to keep in mind.

The area around Pai is beautiful, as the town is set in a green valley surrounded by mountains in the distance and flanked by a small river. Aside from the landscape and despite Pai's popularity, there really is not much to see in Pai itself.

Hiking and Rafting

Although it's tempting to spend your time in Pai just hanging out and enjoying the natural scenery and the people-watching, there are plenty of hiking and rafting trips to be taken whether you want to spend one day or a full week in the mountains or on the river, or a combination of both. Hiking trips are generally one-to-three-day affairs and usually include some elephant-camp visits and tours of local hill tribe villages. White-water rafting on the Pai River is usually a two-day trip and involves camping. Although any tour agency can arrange this trip, **Thai Adventure Rafting** (tel. 05/369-9111, www.activethailand.com, 2,000B a person/day) is considered the most professional.

Nightlife

Pai is full of bars that cater to both Western tourists and Thai tourists, as well as some that feature live music. As there's not much else to do at night, regardless of the crowd, having a few drinks after dark is a popular pastime in the town.

❲ Bebop (188 Mu 8, Rangsiyanon Rd., tel. 05/369-8046, 7 P.M.–1 A.M. daily), a casual live-music venue, is one of Pai's most long-standing watering holes. The two-story wooden structure is much larger than most of the shophouse-style bars in the center of town. There are nightly live performances of rock, blues, and jazz music and the crowd is generally mixed and relaxed. Bebop is about a 10-minute walk outside of the center of town, but worth the short journey.

Charnon's Bar (Pai-Chiang Mai Rd. across from the gas station, tel. 08/9908-2684, 6 P.M.–1 A.M. daily), run by the friendly and savvy Charnon, is a standout spot for sipping drinks and people-watching. The retro bar is full of funky '70s decor and the crowd tends to be mostly young Thai hipsters on vacation.

The stylish but unassuming **Phu Pai Art Café** (22 Mu 4, Rangsiyanon Rd., tel. 08/4209-8169, 7 P.M.–1 A.M. daily), housed in an old Lanna-style teakwood building, features live music on most nights. Sometimes it's folk, other times it's open mic—be prepared for anything when you arrive. The crowd is lively but doesn't get out of hand, making it a nice place to have a few drinks and relax.

Accommodations

Not surprisingly, you'll find scores of 300B-per-night (or cheaper) guesthouses in Pai, as well as a few small upscale resorts right outside of the center of town that are a great value. Unless you're just looking for a cheap room to stumble into after some late-night drinking at one of the town's many little bars, your best bet is to opt for one of the following.

Baan Pai Village (88 Mu 3, Vieng Tai, tel. 05/369-8152, www.baanpaivillage.com, 500B) has basic bungalows just one minute by foot outside of the center of town. Although not as lavish as the more expensive choices, the location is convenient and the rooms themselves comfortable and well maintained, if a little sparse. This property is a great value, but if you're looking for something a little farther away from the center they also have bungalows available at the **Baan Pai Riverside** a few minutes out of town.

Baan Krating Pai Resort (119 Mu 2, Wiangnua, tel. 05/369-8255, 2,000B) has small individual bungalows set in a rice paddy next to the river. The bungalows look rustic from the outside but on the inside are comfortable and modern. The pool on the property is large and there is a restaurant and bar attached.

Belle Villa Resort (113 Mu 6, Wiangnua, tel. 05/369-8226, 2,500B) is just a ten-minute walk to town but feels worlds away. The individual wooden bungalows in a green rice paddy are as well equipped as modern hotel rooms but far more charming. Each comes with its own small deck and hammock, and there is a small swimming pool and very nice casual restaurant on the premises. The property is exceptionally well kept and clean.

Food

Pai is filled with places to eat, although if you're looking for authentic Thai food or anything more than a casual meal it may be difficult to find. The town's many tourists seem to have brought their appetites from home and plenty of mostly mediocre restaurants serving hamburgers and even Mexican food abound. Upscale restaurants just don't fit in with the town's culture, but if you want something a little nicer, the Belle Villa Resort has a nice restaurant serving typical Thai food, as does Baan Krating Pai Resort.

For inexpensive Thai food, **Duang's Restaurant** (5 Rungsiyanon Rd., tel. 05/369-9101, 10 a.m.–9 p.m. daily, 50B) seems to be everyone's favorite place. The location right in the middle of town can't be beat, and the typical Thai dishes are well made. You'll be in the middle of backpacker central here, though there's no getting around it in Pai.

Angie's Kitchen (Rangsiyanon Rd., tel. 05/369-9093, 50B) is another casual Thai restaurant with a bit of atmosphere. Set in an old wooden house, it's not luxurious, but the meals are good and the environment relaxed even by Pai standards.

Pai Blues Bar & Restaurant (tel. 09/157-6997) has a bit of everything: beer, blues, and breakfast, and it's all done pretty well. The menu is eclectic, with Thai and Western food available, but if you're interested in something different ask for one of the Shan dishes.

For a vegetarian meal, head to **Ginger House** (tel. 08/1345-1286). Just outside of the center of town, it's worth the walk, especially if you're looking for something a little more peaceful than the scene in the center. This little wooden house offers nearly all of the normal Thai dishes—curries, noodles and rice—sans meat products.

Getting There

It's hard to believe but there are now daily **flights** into Pai from Chiang Mai on SGA (www.sga.co.th). If you choose this option you'll be taking the 20-minute journey on a 12-seater Cessna and arriving at a landing strip about three kilometers from the center of town.

From Chiang Mai there are five daily **buses** making the four-hour journey for around 150B. If you have a propensity for motion sickness be warned that this may be an unpleasant ride. There are also five daily buses between Mae Hong Son and Pai. The journey takes around four hours and costs less than 100B.

Driving to Pai from Chiang Mai takes you through some beautiful mountain areas and is a great drive if you're comfortable on that terrain. Take Route 107 north from Chiang Mai until you get to Route 1095, which you'll follow all the way to town.

www.moon.com

DESTINATIONS | ACTIVITIES | BLOGS | MAPS | BOOKS

MOON.COM is all new, and ready to help plan your next trip! Filled with fresh trip ideas and strategies, author interviews, informative blogs, a detailed map library, and descriptions of all the Moon guidebooks, Moon.com is all you need to get out and explore the world—or even places in your own backyard. As always, when you travel with Moon, expect an experience that is uncommon and truly unique.

MAP SYMBOLS

▦	Expressway	⬧	Highlight	✈	Airfield	⚓	Golf Course
▦	Primary Road	○	City/Town	✈	Airport	🅿	Parking Area
▦	Secondary Road	◉	State Capital	▲	Mountain	▲	Archaeological Site
▦	Unpaved Road	⊛	National Capital	✚	Unique Natural Feature	☗	Church
- - - -	Trail	★	Point of Interest			⛽	Gas Station
···········	Ferry	•	Accommodation	🮲	Waterfall	⬭	Glacier
⊷⊷⊷	Railroad	▼	Restaurant/Bar	♠	Park	⬭	Mangrove
▦	Pedestrian Walkway	■	Other Location	▣	Trailhead	▦	Reef
▦	Stairs	▲	Campground	⛷	Skiing Area	▦	Swamp

CONVERSION TABLES

$°C = (°F - 32) / 1.8$
$°F = (°C \times 1.8) + 32$
1 inch = 2.54 centimeters (cm)
1 foot = 0.304 meters (m)
1 yard = 0.914 meters
1 mile = 1.6093 kilometers (km)
1 km = 0.6214 miles
1 fathom = 1.8288 m
1 chain = 20.1168 m
1 furlong = 201.168 m
1 acre = 0.4047 hectares
1 sq km = 100 hectares
1 sq mile = 2.59 square km
1 ounce = 28.35 grams
1 pound = 0.4536 kilograms
1 short ton = 0.90718 metric ton
1 short ton = 2,000 pounds
1 long ton = 1.016 metric tons
1 long ton = 2,240 pounds
1 metric ton = 1,000 kilograms
1 quart = 0.94635 liters
1 US gallon = 3.7854 liters
1 Imperial gallon = 4.5459 liters
1 nautical mile = 1.852 km

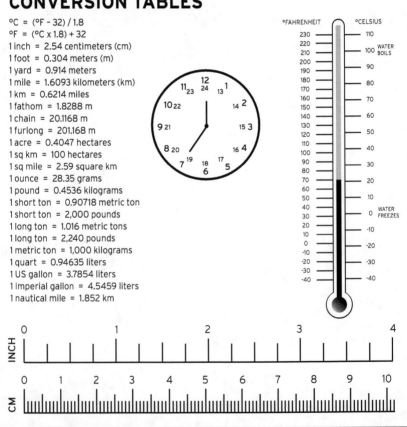

MOON CHIANG MAI
& NORTHERN THAILAND
Avalon Travel
a member of the Perseus Books Group
1700 Fourth Street
Berkeley, CA 94710, USA
www.moon.com

Editors: Grace Fujimoto, Erin Raber
Series Manager: Kathryn Ettinger
Copy Editor: Amy Scott
Graphics Coordinators: Jane Musser, Nicole Schultz
Production Coordinators: Amber Pirker, Jane Musser,
   Lucie Ericksen
Cover Designer: Kathryn Osgood
Map Editor: Brice Ticen
Cartography Director: Mike Morgenfeld
Cartographers: Chris Markiewicz, Lohnes & Wright,
   Kat Bennett, Hank Evans

ISBN-13: 978-1-59880-546-8

Text © 2009 by Suzanne Nam.
Maps © 2009 by Avalon Travel.
All rights reserved.

ABOUT THE AUTHOR

Suzanne Nam

A journalist for one of the world's best-selling magazines, a reformed corporate lawyer, and a dedicated travel writer, Suzanne Nam is as comfortable interviewing Thailand's businessmen and politicians as she is asking a back-alley Chinatown chef for her secret recipe for duck noodles. Her mission is to give travelers the inside information that can turn a good trip to Thailand into a great one. You never know where Suzanne will turn up next. During the next political crisis, listen for her reports on the radio – she files for NPR's *Marketplace* and Fox News Radio. If the surf's up, check for her on the waves of southern Thailand instead.

Like all meaningful things, Suzanne's career was more a product of evolution than of planning. She grew up in Cambridge, Massachusetts. She went to law school after college and practiced law for five years – enough time to produce a rainforest's worth of corporate paperwork. Then she gave it all up to study journalism at Columbia University. The world pulled her east, to London, the Middle East, and finally Bangkok, where she has settled (for now at least). Suzanne's passions include food, photography, books, Bangkok's charismatic street dogs, and above all, writing.